The Klondike's
"Dear Little NUGGET"

Gene Allen. (This photograph was taken some years after the gold rush. From The Klondike Nugget, *by Russell Bankson.)*

The Klondike's "Dear Little *Nugget*"

By
Ian Macdonald
and
Betty O'Keefe

Horsdal & Schubart

Copyright © 1996 by Ian Macdonald and Betty O'Keefe

No part of this book may be reproduced or transmitted in any form by any means, electronic or mechanical, including photocopying and recording, or by any information storage and retrieval system, without written permission from the publisher, except for brief passages quoted by a reviewer in a newspaper or magazine.

Horsdal & Schubart Publishers Ltd.
Victoria, B.C., Canada

Map on page 11 by Tony O'Keefe, Vancouver, BC.

Cover photograph of July 4 celebrations in Dawson City during the gold rush. (Courtesy Vancouver Public Library, photo 9752.) Hand-coloured by Bonnie Curran, Saltspring Island, BC.

Horsdal & Schubart Publishers Ltd. thank The Canada Council for giving financial support to our publishing program.

This book is set in Times.

Printed and bound in Canada by Kromar Printing Limited, Winnipeg.

Canadian Cataloguing in Publication Data

Main entry under title:
The Klondike's dear little Nugget

Includes bibliographical references.
Contains excerpts from The Klondike Nugget.
ISBN 0-920663-45-1

1. Dawson (Yukon)—Social life and customs. 2. Klondike River Valley (Yukon)—Gold discoveries. 3. Yukon Territory—History—1895-1918.* I. Macdonald, Ian, 1928- II. O'Keefe, Betty, 1930- III. Title: Klondike nugget.
FC4047.394.K56 1996   971.9'102   C96-910108-2
F1095.5.D3K56 1996

Contents

The Gold Rush Begins	1
Allen's *Nugget*	5
The Early Editions	17
The American Majority	26
Race Relations	30
Stroller White	32
The Flavour of Dawson	37
Dangerous and Deadly	40
How the World Saw It	42
The Gold Commissioner	45
Hot Dusty Summer	48
Princess of the Yukon	54
Fire	56
In the Fall of 1898	59
Cad Wilson	61
Thanksgiving of a Sort	63
The All-Canadian Route	66
The Dance-Hall Girls	68
Christmas 1898	73
Dawson's Rocket Still Burns Brightly	75
Father William Judge	78

Saloons	81
Joaquin Miller	85
The Final Year of the Century Begins	88
Big Alex	94
Les Girls — A Fact of Life	97
The Consul and the Kicks	99
In the Spring of the Year	103
Alaskan Gold Stampede	106
Charlie Meadows	109
The Telegraph Line Arrives	111
Three Men Executed	114
From Kittens to Mittens	116
Steele of the Northwest Mounted Police	118
The Final Days of '99	120
Christmas Bazaar	123
The Nugget Express	125
The Final Years of the *Nugget*	128
Boom to Bust	144
The *Nugget* Cashes In	147
Endnotes	*151*

Newspapers everywhere ran stories of the gold rush and the trail of '98. Reporters flocked to San Francisco and Seattle, Vancouver and Victoria, some even made it to Skagway and Dawson. It was, however, Gene Allen, an American from Illinois, who arrived first in Dawson with one aim in mind, to publish the town's newspaper. This is the story of Allen, his brother George, and a colourful cast of characters who were portrayed on the pages of *The Klondike Nugget*. This is not an historical perspective, but life as the Allens and the newspaper's reporters saw it in the few short years when Dawson was one of the most exciting places in the world. They lived it and loved it and told it as it was. In the end, like many of the miners who found that fortune trickled through their fingers, the Allens too, lost it all.

THE GOLD RUSH BEGINS

Rugged, ragged, but rich beyond the dreams of most people, the weatherbeaten miners came down the gangplanks of rusty, salt-caked ships at San Francisco and Seattle. Tom Lippy and his wife left the *Excelsior* at the California port struggling under the weight of a great, bulging suitcase. It held 200 pounds of gold, the glistening treasure sought by men since the beginning of time. The Lippys and their companions had lots of it. It was carried in buckskin sacks, cardboard boxes, tin trunks, old jam jars and bottles, cigar boxes and then wrapped in a blanket that two men struggled to carry. Nuggets and gold dust were worth a fortune at a time when an annual income of less than $1,000 was a lot of money. Some of the miners had $100,000 each and more. It is little wonder that excitement raced through the streets and people swarmed to the waterfront to see these men and the fortunes they carried so casually. It was July, 1897, and their arrival triggered the world's greatest gold rush, the Klondike stampede.

Spectators asked where these people came from and were told the Klondike, the Yukon. Where's that? It's a desolate, harsh, long-wintered, icy land thousands of miles to the north in Canada where lie Bonanza, Eldorado and the other creeks that make up the world's richest gold find. It was said to be discovered lying between two layers of gravel like cheese in a sandwich by the prospectors who first struck it rich.

Two tiny ships had carried the gold out for about 1,700 miles down the Yukon River from Dawson to St. Michael, a tiny village at the river mouth. There the cargo was transferred for the 3,000 mile journey down the Pacific Coast. News wires carried the story to the world, telling of this remote land, this Eldorado, and the fabulous wealth waiting there to be plucked from the earth.

There had been reports filtering out for weeks of the fortunes that lay in the Klondike. In fact, the original report by the Canadian government went largely unnoticed. It was the sight of the miners, the nuggets and the dust that sent get-rich-quick fever soaring.

Two days after the arrival of the Lippys there was a wild scene at Schwabacher's Dock in Seattle when the second ship to arrive, the frail, little steamer *Portland*, came in from the north. Five thousand excited people jammed the dock. Wells Fargo's rifle-bearing guards stood at the ready. Newspaper stories had whipped up the frenzy by talking about the arrival of a "Ton of Gold." Actually, it was two tons. In Seattle, one miner who had gone north two years before on a borrowed $300 grubstake had a sack and two bags of gold worth $120,000. Gold was then valued at $16 an ounce.

The miners were mobbed and became instant celebrities. Some scattered their money around freely and bought a lot of drinks. They were pestered by beggars, con men, sellers of all sorts of wonderful things, requests for loans, offers of marriage and much shorter relationships. Some had to hire guards to keep away the mobs.

Thousands around the world decided to hit the trail. Men, and some women, left their jobs, their homes, their pulpits, their practices, their companies, their spouses, their families and their sanity as dreams piled on dreams and they caught the madness. It all seemed so simple. Just look at those who had come from the Klondike! But it wasn't. Many were to pay with their investment, their health, and their lives in a hopeless quest.

The first men to come out of the Klondike were, for the most part, experienced prospectors and miners who had toiled for years in isolation and endured the hardships of the Yukon. They were not clerks, shop assistants or professional men who had never swung a pick or mucked in a narrow shaft or hacked through the frozen earth in search of gold-bearing gravel from ancient streams.

It is estimated that from around the world, but mostly from the United States and Canada, some 100,000 people actually left their homes for the trail. About 30,000 got to Dawson and the creeks at the height of the rush in '97 and '98, most of them suffering the agonies of conquering the Chilkoot and White passes, the mountain barriers between the Pacific Coast and the Yukon.

They died in avalanches, falls, and suicides, from malnutrition, exhaustion, scurvy, typhoid and other diseases and from lack of care and attention. They were preyed upon along the trail by the crooks who had flocked to the scene and by a few hardy prostitutes who plied their trade in tents along the way. In Dawson they found the saloons packed, the pianos plunking, the girls dancing, and the lucky scattering their nuggets and dust. Many quickly realized how impossible their dreams had been. They had reached Dawson, they had joined the brotherhood of the sourdoughs of the trail, but were incapable and in no position to hunt for gold. Many arrived completely broke.

The newcomers found that the first prospectors and miners had staked most of the best claims. Working for them when demand was high was worth $15 a day, but it was back-breaking work done in the grip of the Yukon winter, sometimes at 50 degrees below zero (Fahrenheit). Many stayed only a few days in Dawson, idling on the dusty, crowded main street along with thousands of others before heading back. Many seemed not too disappointed. They hadn't made a fortune but they had challenged the trail to Dawson; they had overcome the miseries and the barriers, the deprivation and the hunger.

In what was for many a miserable tent city, with the scream of sawmills cutting up green lumber 24 hours a day in the background, they had witnessed great wealth amidst grinding poverty.

Only a few became fabulously wealthy, or even marginally rich, and many of these couldn't hold onto their money. Big Alex McDonald, dubbed "The King of the Klondike," and estimated at one time to be worth $20,000,000 died nearly broke.

Among the disappointed must have been the man who packed a deep-sea diver's suit complete with metal helmet and underwater equipment over the passes in the belief that all he had to do was walk along the river and creek bottoms scooping up nuggets. Equally disappointed must have been those who brought custom-made reinforced canvas bags to carry home the gold they expected to collect in a couple of weeks.

The Mounties, the scarlet-coated men of the Northwest Mounted Police, kept out most of the violent lawlessness that was part of other raw mining towns and stampedes. They tolerated much, as Dawson attracted its share of characters, crooks, con men, girls, hustlers, gamblers, drinkers and all the others who appeared on the broad, colourful canvas that the gold city presented to the world.

Like the wealth that slipped so easily through so many fingers, Dawson's heyday didn't last. It was little more than a year between the the time when the main body of the stampeders arrived after the ice had moved out of the lakes and rivers in June, 1898, until some began to leave following word of another great gold strike at Nome, Alaska. Dawson was a spectacular rocket that soared into the Yukon sky with much sound and colour and then fell quickly to earth.

Much has been written about '98 and the people who made the trip. There are many famous names. There were also the not-so-famous whose exploits, wins, losses, tragedies and triumphs contributed to the era.

There were several newspapers that flourished and folded during Dawson's time in the sun at the turn of the century, but none was more colourful, more feisty, more compassionate for the underdog, more combative or more ready to take on officialdom than the *Klondike Nugget*, the first paper in Dawson, as claimed by its co-founder and driving force, Gene Allen. It started as a simple bulletin pinned to a board. It went weekly, semi-weekly, daily, and then, like so much in Dawson, it went bust; so did Allen.

During its life the *Nugget* covered the fabric and style of the times when Dawson was full of life and vitality. Its pages are every-day history, written at the time, without second guessing or professorial analysis. This is how Allen and his staff saw life and lived it as the 20th century dawned on the world.

This is primarily the story of Gene Allen and the *Nugget* for the year and a half that he controlled it and how, in his own right, he became a colourful and important personality in Dawson.

It is fortunate that the Allens, both Gene and his brother George who succeeded him as publisher, carefully kept copies of every edition. These newspapers along with Gene's personal papers were subsequently presented to the library of the University of Washington in Seattle.

ALLEN'S *NUGGET*

THE KLONDIKE NUGGET   July 17, 1898
                    Editorial
There is no color like the glitter of virgin gold, no music like the tinkle of nuggets upon a gold scale, no place where eye and ear alike can be so satisfied as in the Klondike diggings.

§

It was the year before he heard the tinkle of gold that Gene Allen became fascinated with news from the Klondike and the opportunity it offered a young man. In his early 30s, he was ambitious with a burning desire to become part of this great adventure that broke late in the 19th century. A graduate of the University of Kansas, he learned the printing trade in the Midwest. He had suffered through years of a dreary depression and was almost broke. In Seattle, Gene's older brother Pliny Allen was manager of the Metropolitan Printing Company and offered Gene a job as a salesman working on commission. The picture was a little brighter, but not much. Metropolitan was a new company having a tough time in the money scarce Pacific Northwest.

Slightly built, sharp featured and full of nervous energy that made him fidgety, Gene Allen could hardly contain himself when he witnessed the scene at Schwabacher's Dock as men from the north came down the gangplanks with their treasures.

With Gene on the dock was a fellow employee at Metropolitan, Zach Hickman, a man of similar age and ambition who had a small interest in the company but in reality was as financially strapped as Allen. Along with thousands of others they watched and dreamed of Dawson and the Klondike, land of gold dust and nuggets and wealth for all.

Allen was a man who loved the shine of the spotlight and enjoyed being the centre of attention and praise. He wanted to hear the cheers accorded those who, for however short a time, had become champions and fighters for rights. He was an opportunist, a shrewd assessor of possibilities, even if his ambition eventually outreached his plans.

He turned to Hickman, commented that the Klondike was the key to their future, and urged, "Let's get started." Even with all the excitement in the air, the two friends agreed that they wouldn't dig or swing a pick for their gold: they would print it. They both knew the printing business and correctly predicted there would be thousands of people in the remote north hungry for news of the outside world, as well as new businesses with printing needs. Financing the project was the first stumbling block. The two approached Gene's brother Pliny, pointing out the possibilities, including the fact that money was plentiful in Dawson and prices were high. A five cent glass of beer sold for 50 cents in Dawson so surely a newspaper could also be sold at an inflated price.

Pliny listened to the arguments, which were bolstered by the gold that arriving miners were throwing around Seattle and by the general mood of optimism which prevailed along the whole Pacific coast. He finally agreed that Metropolitan would have a 50% interest in the venture while Allen and Hickman would hold 25% each. The bankroll was about $12,000.

That was the beginning of the *Klondike Nugget*, the scrappiest, liveliest, most colourful little paper to take its place in Klondike history. It was a part of the story itself, a player on the crowded stage that was Dawson and the creeks. It was never daunted. Once when the supply of newsprint ran out, the *Nugget* was printed on brown paper originally earmarked for bags and wrapping. The enterprising owners scooped it up and the presses ran.

Planning was a major part of their success in reaching Dawson quickly in good shape to begin business. It was decided that Hickman would make an initial reconnaissance trip to the Klondike. He left Seattle in the middle of August 1897 within a month of signing the financing agreement. Travelling light and alone he assessed their needs: most importantly, how they would get the printing plant over the passes and into Dawson. With a dog team and sled he made the return trip over the frozen rivers and the rough, snowy trails, returning to Seattle in January, 1898.

For $610 Allen and Hickman acquired a printing operation which included a light press for commercial job work, a portable flatbed press, type, and enough paper stock for a year. They also purchased enough food for three men for a year, leaving them the grand sum of about $600 to reach Dawson and start the paper. They picked up ten dogs to haul their sleds, bought in a frenzied market where any mutt was commanding big money. Their choices proved slightly better than most of their fellow stampeders who selected animals entirely unsuitable and useless as sled dogs. They also trained the dogs for a couple of weeks in Seattle before their departure. Then they persuaded two new members to join the venture. They were Allen's 22-year-old, younger brother, George, who gave up school teaching in Everett for the trail, and a relative of Hickman's, named Ed Brandt.

On February 9, 1898, Gene and George Allen boarded the *City of Seattle* for the trip north. Their ship was jam-packed with 600 stampeders, one third more than its legal capacity. Hickman and Brandt followed a few days later with the dogs. The ships were part of one of the

The City of Seattle, *the ship Gene and George Allen boarded on February 9, 1898, for the trip to Skagway. (COURTESY VANCOUVER PUBLIC LIBRARY, PHOTO 32303.)*

strangest armadas of broken-down boats ever to sail and they steamed the foggy, not-too-well-charted coasts of British Columbia and Alaska. The world had been scoured quickly for anything that would float. Old tubs that had been abandoned for years were pushed into service and headed north. Most were overloaded with passengers prepared to pay anything for passage. Some carried five and six times the normal load. Terrified animals, packed into lower decks, suffered terribly. Amazingly, there were relatively few wrecks and little loss of life.

The greatest disaster was the sinking of the *Clara Nevada*, loaded with passengers and a large cargo of dynamite, although it was against the law to carry both people and explosives on the same ship. It blew up on the leg between Skagway and Juneau with the loss of 65 lives. Passengers in other ships travelling the Lynn Canal in that February of 1898 reported having seen in the distance a ship apparently on fire and then hearing the roar of an explosion. About ten days after she left Skagway, the wreckage of the *Clara Nevada* was found scattered along a beach near Seward City. There were no survivors. On February 12 as the *City of Seattle* sailed by Fort Wrangell in heavy snow, Allen wrote in his diary: "Here we were told of the sinking of the steamer Clara Nevada with the loss of all aboard.... We also saw the wreck of the steamer Corona. My nerves are shaking."

Allen and his party landed at Skagway, a new, totally lawless community controlled by Jefferson "Soapy" Smith and his band of cut-throat robbers. Life was cheap in Skagway which was the main take-off point for the White Pass, about 25 miles away.

Any stampeder who failed to attend strictly to business fell into the clutches of Soapy and his gang of crooks. In the book, *The Klondike Nugget*, published in 1935, Allen told his biographer, Russell Bankson: "Every conceivable medium for parting the stampeder from his coin was working full blast. The dance halls were filled with women who were exerting every wile to get their share. Gambling halls with their crooked card games, faro banks and roulette wheels took their slice. If anything was left, the thugs, the strong-arm artists, and the downright murderers made the final cleaning." Allen described Skagway as the "boiling point of Hell."[1]

Smith was a native Georgian who liked to adopt the style of the Southern gentleman. But Soapy definitely was no gentleman; he had been a crook from an early age, moving across the U.S. from boom town to boom town. The Klondike gold rush drew him like a magnet. Over the years Soapy had acquired some friends in high places and he courted them carefully. Despite this the anger of the citizens boiled over and

Smith was killed in a shoot-out on a Skagway wharf July 8, 1898, by the leader of a vigilante group, Frank Reed, who died from wounds inflicted by Soapy's rifle.

In their brief stay in Skagway, months before Soapy met his fitting end, the Allens were appalled by the number of bunco artists in the community and they probably missed some of them. Here they were exposed for the first time to the cold of an arctic winter, the bitterest weather either of them had ever known, and because of it death from pneumonia stalked the trail to Dawson.

One of the many problems encountered by the would-be gold seekers was the age and physical condition of many older men who had spent much of their lives in offices, factories and stores. They were unfit for the rigours of below-zero temperatures, howling blizzards, walking, climbing, manhandling supplies and pulling sleds when dogs died or proved useless.

Because of a new requirement of the Canadian authorities, that a ton of supplies must accompany anyone heading to Dawson, goods were moved in small amounts and cached along the way. On the passes, a stampeder could carry little more than 50 pounds on his back and so he must return again and again for another load. It made the climb seem unending. This regulation had not been in effect when Hickman made his earlier scouting trip.

Allen noted that many stampeders wore heavy clothing unsuited for the trail, but Hickman's information from his initial trip proved valuable and they wore lighter clothing. Their equipment and food had also been carefully selected. They had a Yukon wood-burning stove, good tents, blankets and fur robes. They carried a well-balanced selection of canned and other non-perishable foods. Along the trail there were hunters selling fresh moose meat and grayling, trout, whitefish and salmon.

The group elected to go over the White Pass. The alternate route was over the Chilkoot Pass, shorter but steeper, reached via the town of Dyea on the opposite shore of the Lynn Canal. The Mounties controlled movement over both passes, charging import duties on some goods and backing up their authority with weapons. The weapons were never fired, even though the import taxes irked many Americans.

Disturbing news reached the small party only ten days out of Skagway. A traveller told Gene Allen there was another group heading for Dawson with a printing plant and plans to start a paper. As the desire to be the first paper in Dawson was a major goal, the four men picked up the pace, battling the coldest bite of winter and the most rugged part of the trail without rest. Some of the dogs died and they were soon down to one team but Allen was able to purchase a horse from a stampeder who took ill and gave up. Anything that might help to move supplies was used on the trail, from oxen to a team of reindeer that also proved absolutely useless and was eventually sold by the owner for food.

After a month the four men from Seattle hauled the last of their supplies over the White Pass. They had travelled only 30 miles from Skagway and the Klondike was still 600 miles away.

Allen and Hickman had planned to reach the head of Lake Bennett, cut lumber and build a boat, and then to take the water route to Dawson when spring arrived and the ice went out. They now discussed the need for one of them to go on ahead and set up in Dawson so everthing would be ready to roll when the presses finally arrived. Ahead lay a lot of dangerous water, rapids and sand bars on a route known to sourdoughs then as via Bennett Lake, Tagish and Marsh lakes, to Fifty Mile River, Miles Canyon, Whitehorse Rapids, Lake LaBarge, Thirty Mile River, Lewes River and finally into the Yukon River and the last leg to Dawson.

It would be difficult to make a speedy trip under the conditions that prevailed, but Gene Allen was lucky. He met an old friend from Seattle who was also in a hurry. Joe Dizzard had heard of a new gold strike on Walsh Creek near Big Salmon River and he was anxious to check it out. Both Allen and Dizzard wanted to hurry on ahead and so a pact was struck: they would head out together and the remaining members of both parties would join forces and wait for breakup when travel by barge along the lakes and rivers would be possible. A day was spent putting together the equipment and supplies needed by Allen and Dizzard, placing the emphasis on lightness and speed. They had a small stove, bedding, tent, clothing and food for three dogs and two men for 60 days. The load weighed less than 500 pounds and was carried on a single sled. Allen and Hickman split up what was left of their stake: it came to $30; their dreams and hopes depended on exactly $15 each. They were out in the wilds, almost 600 miles from their destination, facing treacherous and mostly unknown waters, with the goal of reaching Dawson and getting into business on a total of $30.

The task ahead called for all of Allen's hustle, talent and entrepreneurial spirit. Dizzard was comparatively wealthy: he had $30. On March 17, with a howling wind and a temperature of 25 below, they set out. They faced a considerable danger with the coming of spring. Ice on the lakes and rivers was starting to weaken as the sun shone and temperatures climbed, but they had to risk it if they were to keep ahead of the main group on the trail and the opposition. They were never quite sure who was in the lead.

"Dear Little Nugget"

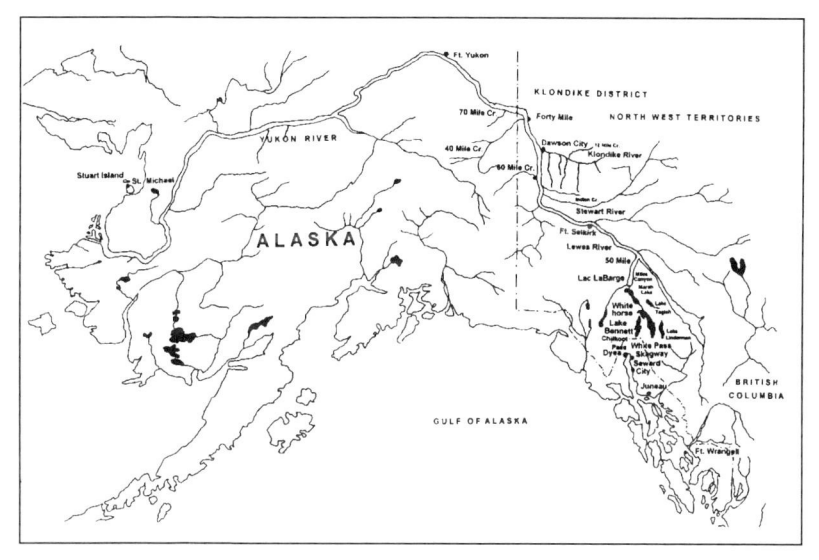

The Allen party went from Skagway through the White Pass to Lake Bennett, and down the Yukon River to Dawson City.

On April 8, Allen wrote in his diary, "The ice on Fifty Mile is almost impassable. It is giving out like rotten cloth, and every step we had to watch that we did not plunge to death through an air pocket or a rotten spot. Several times during the day we were caught on floating cakes of ice. There's a thrill for you. Little Liza had nothing on us. A loaded sled, three dogs and two men marooned on a floating cake of ice with swirling, icy water all around us. But each time we made connections with solid ice and were able by swift action to race to safety on solid shore ice."

Adventure piled on adventure and there was more than one scary experience for the pair as they covered the miles to Dawson. On April 10 Allen was struck with snow blindness so they were forced to rest until he could see again and the pain in his eyes lessened.

There were a few expenses along the way and by early May, Allen had less than two dollars left and not much food. He had to be careful in his dealings with the Mounties who were always prepared to turn back anyone who appeared not to have the means of support that would be needed in Dawson. With a great influx of people, supplies were running short in the gold town and the start of the navigation season, when stocks would be replenished by river transport, was still weeks away.

The Mounties were trying to enforce strict conditions on the lakes and rivers to avoid a possible heavy death toll as thousands of inexperienced men tried frantically to get to Dawson. Men who never built a boat before were willing to risk their lives in roaring rivers and rapids in craft quickly put together from raw lumber and rudimentary plans, or often no plans at all. The Mounties were not numerous and they were trying to exercise control over hundreds of miles of water route. There were some gold seekers who died in the chilling, swirling waters. The exact number of those who perished has never been determined, but in light of the thousands involved and the circumstances, the toll was much less than it might have been. The young policemen of the Yukon were superb.

A combination of fast thinking, shrewdness, meeting old friends and more than a touch of luck saw Allen making deals for passage as they moved along. He convinced one group that he and Dizzard were experienced rivermen in order to earn their passage on a barge, although handling the heavy sweeps of their craft for the first time brought them to exhaustion. Gradually the miles passed by. The last stretch was on the barge *Black Maria*. The police owned half of the craft and Allen had befriended the young owner of the other half who was willing to give them transport providing the Mounties didn't object. It was here that Allen ran into a Mountie with an entrepreneurial spirit and perhaps the only one with a bent for trying to make a little cash on the side.

When Allen and Dizzard compared notes they found that the Mountie had stipulated a $100 fare to cover passage for two. Then he tried to collect it from both of them. They agreed to pay him at a later date although they had no means of meeting his demands. They helped load the barge for the policemen over the next few days in payment for their passage but carefully avoided the Mountie in question. They had found he actually had no authority on the craft and had not been assigned to go with the flotilla to Dawson. In charge of the move was Major James Walsh, who was unaware of the attempted scam by one of his men. When the order finally came to push off, Allen and Dizzard were more than happy to help shove the *Maria* into the river and leap aboard, leaving the scarlet-coated, would-be entrepreneur standing alone on the beach without $100 from either of them.

Knowing at this time that he and Dizzard were running ahead of the main fleet and that he was ahead of his rivals, Allen relaxed on the final run to Dawson. Dizzard disembarked at Big Salmon River to wait for his friends, having learned by this time that there was no new gold strike. The trials of the trail and the wild waters were over for Allen, the Mounties were out in front. Tuesday, May 17, 1898, was the end of the long, long journey that had had its beginnings in Seattle. About four o'clock in the afternoon Klondike City, less romantically and popularly known as Lousetown, was sighted and Allen got off.

"Dear Little Nugget"

For the first time during his long trek, he felt alone in a strange land. He cooked up what was left of his dwindling supplies and was making some beans on the beach when he heard a voice. It demanded: "Answer me this, pard, are you or ain't you the missing link?" As he later recalled, in discussions with Russell Bankson, the voice belonged to one of two men who seemed to find him a curiosity. Largely unwashed after several months on the trail and sporting a bushy, long, red beard, he must have seemed a wild man to the strangers on the beach. He realized then he hadn't had a shave or a haircut since Skagway several months earlier. One of his new acquaintances said, "You better get yourself trimmed up or someone's goin' to put you in a zoo an' charge to have a look."

Allen replied, "Have your fun and likewise have some beans. And on top of that, tell me how you go about getting located here."

They told him he certainly didn't want to stay in Lousetown, which was indeed a lousy place. It derived its reputation from being where the first old sourdoughs had their camp. Their health habits left much to be desired and now every boat and human that touched shore was immediately host to the large local louse population.

Allen had exactly $1.65 in his pocket, and decided he might as well make a minor splash and buy them a drink as he accepted their invitation to walk into Dawson. He spotted a saloon: "I emptied my pockets of every cent I had and three small whiskey were set before me. The bartender took $1.50 and I pocketed the 15 cents... that was my introduction to Dawson City."

Like all who saw the teeming scene, Allen's first sight of Dawson produced memories for a lifetime. The crowds wandered aimlessly on the rough streets, amid the tents, the two-and-three-storey buildings and the stores and offices hurriedly thrown up and built from raw lumber. He heard the screams of sawmills producing the building material so urgently wanted, all of it happening even under the midnight sun of the Yukon.

Allen quickly explored the town and went out to the creeks to see where the wealth was being torn from the ground. Again an old friendship paid off. He went in search of a Seattle man, Alf Byers. He walked about 15 miles to reach the claim on Bonanza Creek where Byers and partners had struck it rich. Allen worked for a day shoveling gold-bearing gravel into a sluice box and watching how the gold was recovered. His friend tossed about $100 worth of dust into a sack and presented it to Allen. He had another grubstake and could continue with his plans.

Despite watching Byers and his partners and their gold, Allen didn't catch gold fever but stuck to his original plan to make his money from publishing and printing. There was nothing in his subsequent life to suggest that he even quietly invested in any claims. After Dawson, he was never a rich man.

Allen soon found a site for his paper and again was lucky as another Seattle friend, George Trew, loaned him $200 to secure it. How he actually got the land was due to his brash, fast-talking style. It was a junk-filled, vacant lot, only 18 by 20 feet but still a valuable piece of property in booming Dawson. Judge Morford, formerly of Yakima, Washington, was the resident agent for the owners. Amused by the style and confidence of Allen he told him that if he had enough ambition to clear the dump to go to it and he could have the site rent free. It took him nearly as long to clear the site as it did to construct a building to house his paper, about a week, but by June 7 everything was ready and awaiting the arrival of the presses.

As these preparations were taking place and with success almost within his grasp, Allen learned that the opposition was running ahead of Hickman. The news simply spurred him on to produce his first copy of the *Klondike Nugget* on Friday, May 27, 1898. It was a collection of town gossip and other items of news he was able to pick up, typed on a sheet of paper and pinned to a pole in the middle of town. Soon the pole was surrounded by news-hungry men pushing and shoving to read the sheet of paper. The *Nugget* was in business. The opposition, the *Yukon Midnight Sun* rolled its presses first, but Allen always stuck to his claim that his typed, stuck-on-the-pole *Nugget* was Dawson's first newspaper, and there were few who ever argued the point. He kept changing the

Front Street, Dawson City, in June, 1898, just after the "Dear Little Nugget*" began. (COURTESY VANCOUVER PUBLIC LIBRARY, PHOTO 9792.)*

news on his board as it came in and the crowds came, even when the Yukon River flooded and they stood knee deep in water to read it. Allen hired salesmen to hustle subscriptions and job-printing orders. An annual subscription was $24 or an ounce-and-a-half of gold. He had 400 subscribers signed up before the plant arrived. Advertising was sold for ten dollars an inch and there were lots of takers for the as yet unseen paper from the press. On June 10 Hickman arrived with the precious press undamaged and in good working condition. Six days later, the newly installed press produced its first edition.

Allen paid good money to his employees; $15 a day to compositors and $400 a month to other staff. He also bought, at premium prices, any newspaper a new arrival brought in. A two-month-old story was still news and readable in a community without any regular links to the outside. Allen battled nose to nose with the opposition and contacted incoming passengers on boats before they actually reached Dawson in order to buy papers and rush them to his plant where the news was rewritten and printed in the *Nugget*.

Typical of the style of the *Nugget* was its crackerjack "newsboy," 65-year-old "Uncle Andy Young," unquestionably Dawson's oldest vendor. Andy, a Scottish immigrant, was a hustler and told Allen that age didn't matter. He quickly sold an initial 25 copies provided to him and became a popular sight on Dawson streets and in the saloons and dancehalls, shouting - "The *Nugget*! The *Nugget*! The Dear Little *Nugget*!" He also trusted his customers and was often heard to say, "If you ain't got the price, pay me later, but take the *Nugget* now." Soon he had control of sales in the city, subcontracting to other newsboys. "Uncle Andy" died tragically one night, however, when his cabin burned to the ground, the fire probably started by an overturned lamp. The *Nugget* ensured he was buried with style and many of his customers paid their last respects to the irrepressible little man who had helped put the "Dear Little *Nugget*" on the Dawson scene.

Dawson authorities and some of the growing business and commercial interests found nothing terribly "dear" about the *Nugget* as time went on. Readers liked the paper's racy style and the miners, or most of them, loved the *Nugget*'s role in supporting their causes. Allen basked in his role as crusader, but he was far from loved by the majority of authorities who saw him as a trouble-making, antagonistic Yankee with no respect for Canadian law and a scandal monger to boot. Allen knew that his main market lay with the miners and he started out immediately to voice their many complaints and frustrations and push their interests. There were great crusades, including the sponsoring of a deputation with a petition to

Ottawa complaining about restrictive regulations and unfair taxation. The delegation grabbed headlines as people became intrigued by this message from the far-away gold city, and the journey which began in Dawson with dogs and a sled in the grip of winter.

In the short span of its existence, the *Nugget* chronicled in a lively and frequently fearless way, with scant attention to the laws of libel, the daily lives of those who had made the northern trek — their triumphs and tragedies, successes and failures, and their pride in being sourdoughs of the trail. The *Nugget* told the stories of the people of Dawson, but the paper itself was also a vital part of the overall story of the times, of the most publicized gold rush in the world.

THE EARLY EDITIONS

The *Nugget* began on May 27 on a pole and published from June 16, 1898, to July 14, 1903, off the presses. During its first few weeks of publication, to the end of June, 1898, these were some of the stories that appeared on the pole or in print.

THE KLONDIKE NUGGET   May 27, 1898
         Vol. 1, No. 1, Dawson City, North West Territory
           The First Newspaper to be Published in Dawson

Until our plant arrives items of interest which may come under our notice will be bulletined from day to day. It is hoped that we may be of some benefit to the greatest mining camp in the world, and that the venture may prove of slight benefit to the publishers.

     E. C. Allen, Business Manager
     G. E. Storey, Chief of Staff

§

G. E. Storey was another old friend from Seattle, a composing room foreman from a newspaper where Allen had worked. When the two met in Dawson and Storey learned presses were on the way he became one of Allen's first employees, an unpaid one for the first few weeks.

THE KLONDIKE NUGGET   May, 1898
Police Gazette Tabooed
Early this morning a stalwart constable might have been seen walking along the waterfront with about 26 copies of Richard E. Fox's famous publication under his arm. Inquiry developed the fact that they were not for sale but had been confiscated under a law which prohibits selling and passing through customs literature of an obscene and immoral character.

§

THE KLONDIKE NUGGET   June, 1898
Editorial
That gold will be discovered beyond the dreams of avarice is already an assured fact. The world has already been stricken dumb with the marvellous tales of fabulous riches that have come down from the Klondike district....Enough truth has been gleaned ...to warrant the statement that gold fields on the face of the earth today excel in extent and wealth those of the Northwest Territory and Alaska....

There are other sources of wealth in this remarkable country besides the gold fields. There are untold quantities of silver, of copper, of lead, and iron yet waiting to be brought to light, while coal beds are certain to be discovered ere long. Oil has already been discovered. There are forests to be cut down and fisheries to be developed; in fact, the country is filled with resources only awaiting the brain and muscle of man to be turned into wealth.

§

Among the prospectors, would-be prospectors and miners in the Klondike, there were more than a few would-be poets. They mined the language with enthusiasm but there was little that was golden. These dabblers in verse found the *Nugget* was a ready market for their work, particularly if it had a humorous touch. The following piece headed, "Just from Dawson," was among the first. It told the sad tale of a mining man, "froze solid p.d.q." who was despatched to his home in Deadwood, South Dakota.

THE KLONDIKE NUGGET   June, 1898
Just from Dawson
A Dawson City mining man lay dying on the ice,
He didn't have a woman nurse - he didn't have the price

A comrade kneeled beside him as the sun sank in repose
To listen to his dying words and watch him while he froze.

The dying man propped up his head above four rods of snow,
And said I never saw it thaw at ninety-eight below.
Send this little pin-head nugget that I swiped from Jason Dills,
To my home, you know, at Deadwood, Deadwood in the Hills.

Tell my friend, and my enemies, if you ever reach the East,
That this Dawson City region is no place for man or beast;
That the land's too elevated, and the wind too awful cold,
And the Hills of South Dakota yield as good a grade of gold.

Tell my sweetheart not to worry with sorrow too intense,
For I would not thus have panned out had I a lick of sense.
Oh! The air is growing thicker, and those breezes give me chills,
Gee, I wish I was in Deadwood, in Deadwood in the Hills.

Tell the fellows in the homelands to remain and have a cinch,
That the price of patent pork chops here is eighty cents an inch,
That I speak as one who's been here, scratching 'round to find the gold,
And at ten per cent of discount I could not buy a cold.

Now, so long, he faintly whispered, I have told you what to do.
And he closed his weary eyelids and froze solid p.d.q;
His friends procured an organ box and c.o.d.'d the bills,
And sent the miner home that night to Deadwood in the Hills.

§

The pages of *The Klondike Nugget* carefully chronicled the serious concerns of the population of Dawson as well as the escapades of the citizens themselves, sometimes serious, often humorous.

THE KLONDIKE NUGGET   June, 1898
Thirsty Dawson
Men with money to buy whiskey, and no whiskey for sale, was the serious condition of affairs which confronted the inhabitants of Dawson only a short time ago. It was indeed a sad sight to see some of the old-timers walk up to the bar and call for a lemonade with a far-away look in their eyes, and the apologetic manner in which their orders were filled by the accommodating barkeeper was enough to

convince an onlooker that unless relief arrived soon, serious complications would soon arise.

On Monday night, May 31, the Opera House saloon was opened and five barrels of good whiskey came to light. In less than six days the smiling attendants would shock the prospective regalers with the remark: "We have no whiskey. What will you drink?"

The 16 barrels brought in by the May West were emptied at $1 per drink, but the recent arrival of boats from above the cargo of the Weare have placed Dawson in her normal conditions, and we now have plenty of liquid refreshments and are willing to let the future take care of itself.

§

THE KLONDIKE NUGGET　　　　　　　　　　　　　　　June, 1898

Calamity Jane

Calamity Jane, of Deadwood and Leadville fame, and one of Wells-Fargo's most trusted detectives, is in Dawson. The life of this woman has been filled with wild adventures and on more than one occasion she has been forced to take human life in defense of her own; yet a kinder, truer character would be hard to find.

In upholding the law and defending what is right, she is braver than most men and at the same time, in manner and deportment, she is as gentle and refined as any of her Eastern sisters. There is a suggestion in the steel-blue eyes, however, that would warn the unwary, and a glance at the half-sad face indicates that her life has not been all sunshine.

§

THE KLONDIKE NUGGET　　　　　　　　　　　　　　　June, 1898

Bill Gates Lives

Despite a three-column obituary in the Seattle Post-Intelligencer, Mr. Swiftwater Bill Gates is still well and alive. Mr. Gates reached Dawson in safety some time ago.

§

Swiftwater Bill had to live, he had to exist. He couldn't be a character in fiction, a figment of some writer's imagination. His exploits kept the Yukon, and everywhere else in the world that heard of him, chuckling and wondering what to expect next from this jaunty, natty, little man, possibly the Klondike's greatest character. This was no mean feat in a place, and an era, where the outrageous was the ordinary, where a tiny part of the world lived its own bizarre, wild, lavish life, all of it sparkling and dusted with gold.

Swiftwater's nerve, his verve, his many marriages — he married often and he liked them young — and his ability to pick himself up from disaster, to go on to one venture after another was the stuff of great tales of the trail of '98 and the Klondike.

There was always the question of what was true and what was blarney, but there was enough that was seen and well known to establish the reality of Swiftwater and his deeds. Bill was a small man, about five feet five, with a long, untidy black moustache. His background was a bit obscure, however, and few believed his tales of being an experienced boatman on many rivers as he followed the gold trail in the U.S. and earned the nickname, Swiftwater.

His early days in the Yukon were far from glamorous. He was a dishwasher for a spell at Forty Mile, and was among the first to rush to Dawson when news of the strike broke. Soon he was in the money, decked in a style of dress he wore until the day he died which included a plug hat and a Prince Albert coat. Happy-go-lucky, he saw his money come and go. One night in '97, spectators watched as Bill gambled and lost $500 in a few minutes. He also lavished his charm and his money on the dance-hall girls. Nineteen-year-old Gussie Lamore was an early favourite and because she said she liked eggs, stories abounded about Bill buying up all he could of the scarce commodity at a dollar each to bestow on his love; she was already married but declared she was prepared to wed him.

Bill loved gold, but didn't want to sweat for it or get his hands dirty. He teamed up with a promoter, Jack Smith, which led to the opening of Dawson's most famous premises, the Monte Carlo dance hall and saloon. It could have been viewed as sending the fox to look after the chickens, but it was agreed that Bill would go to San Francisco to acquire the furnishings for the pleasure palace; nothing was too good for the Monte Carlo and the entertainers that would be needed. Many thought Smith had lost both his mind and his money, but Swiftwater did return, his mission completed, although there is no denying he had lived life to the full while he was in California. Swiftwater enjoyed the limelight and got word to Dawson in early '98 that he was on his way back. Everyone expected a show and they weren't disappointed. Along with furnishings for the Monte Carlo and a good supply of whiskey, he brought 20 to 30 show girls.

Gene Allen recalled the crowd that gathered on the river bank to watch the spectacle. "Late in the afternoon I was standing down close to the river's edge when the outfit was sighted, floating with the current, and a wild cheer went up from the thousands of watchers. In front was a Peterborough canoe and in the prow stood Swiftwater Bill Gates himself, dressed in Prince Albert and high silk hat, his flowing mustache curled back over his shoulders, his chest out, his head up, arms extended to the people of Dawson City. Behind him a beautiful girl sat on top of a keg of whiskey, while the oarsman in the rear deftly piloted the craft in towards the bank. Then followed a scow loaded down with barrels of whiskey, and behind this a second scow fitted up with cabin-like living quarters for the girls who lined the railings in their gay dresses, waving a greeting to the cheering mob. It was a sight which never will be forgotten by the stampeders who witnessed it."[2]

They don't make many showmen like Swiftwater. Many adventures followed; Bill could never concentrate on simply one enterprise and soon he sold out his share in the highly successful Monte Carlo to his partner Smith. His exploits, however, continued to delight *Nugget* readers. There were his marriages to the three Lamore sisters, the legality of which was doubtful, and his love life became more involved as Bill flitted between the Yukon, Alaska and the States. He became enamoured of 17-year-old Kitty Brandon and her mother gave chase after they ran off. This episode resulted in a marriage ceremony in a Washington town. Kitty was his step-niece and actually took the place of another teenager who had caught Bill's eye, Bera Beebe, aged 15. At one point Swiftwater was being pursued by two possible mothers-in-laws, Mrs. Brandon and Mrs. Beebe.

Not surprisingly, Swiftwater eventually was nailed and jailed for bigamy. In some bizarre circumstances, which included his passing out some gold nuggets to officials, Bill got out of these marital problems with no great suffering. The experience barely slowed him down and he stated he was still interested in marriage. Bill again delighted his followers when a very enlightening story appeared, with some very frank comments from an unexpected source. One of his wives, the equally lively Gussie Lamore, a great favourite in the theatres and dance halls, confirmed that she was only the first of the three Lamore girls to marry Swiftwater as they tossed him about like a baseball in the infield. There were some contradictions in her story. It was hard to believe that the free-spending Bill could ever be cheap, but, of course, there were the times when all of his money trickled through his fingers. This is the *Nugget* headline and the story, which appeared, reprinted from a

Spokane paper. Eager readers lapped up news about their favourite character, unsinkable Swiftwater.

THE KLONDIKE NUGGET   June, 1898

Swiftwater Bill Gates
Discussed by One of His
Many Wives Who Says He
Is A Very Cheap Guy
But is Very Jealous

Among the visitors to the city is William C. Gates, who is better known as Swiftwater Bill. Mr. Gates is a noted character of the Klondike gold fields and he has been the hero of many activities, not the least of these was his marriage to Gussie Lamore, variety artist and his subsequent marriage to two of her three sisters.

Gussie was the first Mrs. Gates, then her oldest sister became Mrs. Gates No. 2, next a younger sister became Mrs. Gates No.3. The first Mrs. Gates has resumed her occupation as a vaudeville performer. She is now playing in Spokane and is not a bad looking woman. She has genuine flaxen hair, a piquant expression, a pleasant smile and is neat and stylish in appearance. She is still young and the dissipation incidental to the consumption of champagne which Swiftwater used to buy for her has left no telling marks on her pleasant countenance. She recently unburdened herself to a reporter, revealing details of her sisters' marriages.

"I met him in Dawson in the winter of '97. He certainly had the coin then. He lavished money on me but I got dead sick of the guy. I love eggs and he bought out a whole consignment at $1 each.

"I went outside with Bill and introduced him to our family in Frisco. Well would you believe it but my sister Grace cops him out — steals him from me cold. I get a divorce with alimony and use her as co-respondent. Our family is nothing if not on the square so after I get a divorce Grace marries him.

"She lived with him for a matter of weeks and splits. She couldn't go him at all. Divorced.

"Who steps in and joins up with him, sister Nell! She lives with him for a week. She says she has a divorce from him but I don't believe it.

"About a year ago I read in the paper that he had run away with his niece. He looked up Grace broke and got money. No woman could live with him. He throws his money around, I know about it. He hasn't a particle of intellect and couldn't carry on an interesting conversation for five minutes to save his soul.

"You ought to see his getup. He wears a plug hat of the vintage of '75, then he has a Prince Albert coat and negligee that cost him $1.25. He tops the whole thing off with dancing pumps.

"I have good relations with my sisters. Why should we fall out? Not over that stiff I hope. We simply kept him in the family. When he got tired of one of us we simply passed him along to the next one. If we hadn't some other fairy would have got him. There was no reason why all that coin should not be kept in the Lamore family as long as possible."

§

The years rolled on, the adventures continued, but eventually the world learned that Swiftwater's last caper had ended in Peru with his death in 1935. He was still on the hunt for gold or any other of the earth's treasures and it was said he had sweet-talked his way into a massive silver-mining concession.

Along with its first story on Swiftwater Bill, *The Klondike Nugget* in June 1898 also carried the following items:

THE KLONDIKE NUGGET   June, 1898
Advertisement
Pavilion Theatre Only Show in the City
First Class artists only. Complete change of program weekly.
Crowds greet performers nightly and encore each act.
Best dance floor in the city. First class music.
Everybody dances after the show.
If you want to enjoy yourself thoroughly visit the Pavilion

§

THE KLONDIKE NUGGET   June, 1898
A New Attraction
Last night there was an opening that was a surprise in two ways. First, that the new arrivals could open up for business so soon, and secondly that such talent should find its way to this quarter of the globe. The Oatley Sisters (Polly and Lottie) only arrived here last week, yet last night at the corner of Second Street and Fourth Avenue, they sang to a throng all night long. With spendid voices and the latest songs, and being excellent dancers, they made a decided hit. They danced the buck and wing together in a manner that pleased the admiring spectators. Their dog, Tiny, a mite of a canine, comes in for

his share of praise for he sings a little himself much to the wonderment of everybody.

§

THE KLONDIKE NUGGET   June, 1898
Dogs

We wonder why no one has started a sausage factory in Dawson. There are enough quadrupeds roaming the streets to supply an institution for at least a day.

§

THE KLONDIKE NUGGET   June, 1898
Sunday Closing

Dawson is probably the only mining centre in the world which is a Sunday closing town. Work of any kind is prohibited and all boisterousness on the streets is quickly stopped by the police. Those who have been drunk for a week and gone six days minus sleep are given a chance to sober up and get in condition for another week's run. When the two hands stand on the 12 on Sunday nights, however, there is merrymaking and the rest of the night reminds one of a brewer's picnic back in the States.

§

THE AMERICAN MAJORITY

When the *Nugget*'s account of the U.S. July 4 celebration made page one and in the same edition the account of the July 1 Canadian national day made page 5, it was quite clear where the *Nugget*'s main interest lay outside of Dawson and which audience was most important. The Canadian observance was a staid and formal event, but the opening barrage of gunfire marking July 4 had the town livestock stampeding because of the din, and the police wondering about the amount of weaponry that suddenly appeared.

As part of the celebration there also was a pickup baseball game on the sand bar in front of town, the bats being discarded and broken pieces of boat masts, the balls ranging from twisted twine to rounded blocks of wood.

THE KLONDIKE NUGGET   July, 1898

July 4 Celebration

It was with the wildest enthusiasm the large American population of Dawson welcomed the advent of the Fourth of July. Scarcely had the watch ticked a few seconds after midnight on Sunday when a regular fusilade of pistol shots broke the Sunday stillness, and noise and lots of it became the shrill order of the hour. With hoarse "whoops" and "hellos", every loyal sleeping son of Jonathan jumped from his cot and joined in the general racket.

They sprang from their tents from one end of Dawson to the other end of Klondike City, and proceeded to pierce the air with all kinds of projectiles from an assortment of guns of all kinds in the hands of all kinds of men, but every mother's son of them jubilant of the fact that for the first time in history, the vast Yukon was being awakened from her sleep of centuries and would not forget the day we celebrate even though thousands of miles from home.

§

THE KLONDIKE NUGGET (page 5)　　　　　　　　　　July, 1898
Canadians Celebrate

The Canadian element of Dawson, together with a sprinkling of Englishmen and Americans united on the evening of July 1, in a dinner at the Regina Club Cafe in honor of Dominion Day. The gathering numbered nearly 250 men, presided over by the venerable Judge McGuire. The menu was excellent and the wine list as long as your arm, while the toasts and the responses occupied over three hours in their delivery. The enthusiasm was intense and noisy and could only be vented in hurrahs and occasional choruses of those never-to-be-forgotten college songs.

Our numerous outside readers will be much interested in the menu, for in the outside world we are generally suspected of subsisting on a diet of pork and beans, with an occasional round of shoe leather for a change. The menu was as follows:

Consomme a la Jardiniere; Rockpoint oysters, raw; gherkins; Picilili; lobster cutlets a la Newburg; chicken salad en mayonnaise; broiled moose chops aux champignons; cold tongue; roast beef; boiled ham; Bengal Club chutney; saratoga chips; assorted cakes and jellies; pears; peaches; Edam cheese; cafe.

§

Shortly after the flag-waving and outburst of patriotism inspired by the July 4 holiday, and possibly celebrated with increased enthusiasm because of their distance from home, the Americans of Dawson had something else to cheer about.

It was old news to the rest of the world, but newspapers brought in told of the great American victories in the Philippines and Cuba with the outbreak of the Spanish-American War. The papers were devoured page by page and men crowded around to hear a reader tell of U.S. exploits — those of its navy in particular.

Jingoism hit great heights and there were cheering crowds to watch a band playing Sousa marches lead a parade through the streets of Dawson. The crowd was happy to stand for a long time listening to speeches that were highly charged.

The *Nugget* told its readers of the event:

THE KLONDIKE NUGGET   July, 1898

The Spanish-American War

A dozen or so outside papers as of July 5 were brought into Dawson per lightning express, i.e. by open boat down the Yukon River, containing an account of the annihilation of Cerveca's fleet. The copies had a great impact. Ten thousand loyal Americans and nearly as many deeply-interested Canadians got scent of the glorious news and had to read or hear it read before they could turn their attention to various other matters. A copy of the Times was followed wherever it went by a news-hungry crowd who had to be satisfied.

No one was allowed to read his own copy in peace even though he had paid for it in good Eldorado gold dust and we must acknowledge that none wanted to read it alone either. Papers were divided into sheets and handed around while some good loud-voiced reader was chosen to yell out the paragraphs as they were handed up to him. As late as 11 p.m. there could be seen crowds of a thousand eager men gathered around a reader on Front Street.

Men laughed and shook hands. The general hilarity and good feeling was unusual. In the cities of the States the news was received with fireworks and bombs. I would doubt it was received with any more satisfaction than here.

§

While there was much about Canadian authority and regulations that Allen and his paper didn't like, there was little said in the *Nugget* to create divisiveness in Dawson's population, which was overwhelmingly American. As time went by and harsh conditions persisted, problems or perceived problems began cropping up for the Americans.

The issue that led to a *Nugget* editorial with the heading "Discrimination" was one that continues to bedevil society today — the allocation of resources to meet pressing social needs. The *Nugget* was direct in its remarks, but in its final words was careful to point out that it felt that many Canadians supported its position.

THE KLONDIKE NUGGET   January, 1899

Discrimination

The action of the Yukon authorities in regard to sick Americans is most peculiar to say the least. We are unable to grasp the force of the reasoning in the case of a miner presenting himself to them absolutely destitute and helpless from scurvy and without a friend with money for a single day's medical attendance.

Why that man's nationality should be presumably enquired into and then himself packed off instantly to the American relief committee in case he prove to be an American, we cannot understand.

Americans forked out taxes last year. Out of $2.5 million contributed in taxes last year, and because of the extortions last year, by the 30,000 people of the territory, at least $2 million was contributed by Americans. True, gentlemen, you have expended some $829,000 in relief work, but how insignificant an amount when compared with the whole or compared to the needs of the country.

The Nugget will put itself on record right here and now as unalterably opposed to any kind of discrimination in favor of Canadians; and British, South Africans, Australians and many good Canadians will stand with us on that proposition.

§

RACE RELATIONS

The *Nugget* gave little consideration to the question of race relations or racial prejudice. The temper of the times dictated the language and *Nugget* reporters used stereotyped references to racial origin that would not be tolerated in later years. This was 1898. Racial origin was mentioned frequently in stories of police and court events. Often there was reference to an individual as white, American or Canadian, preferably Protestant or Catholic, and the point was invariably made if the individual did not fall into these categories. In one opening performance at the Grand Hotel, the headliner sang a song entitled:" All Coons Look Alike to Me."

This attitude was reflected in an early editorial dealing with international affairs. It was made clear who was superior in the world.

THE KLONDIKE NUGGET   June, 1898
Editorial

When John Bull and Uncle Sam stand shoulder to shoulder the rest of the world must take off its hat. The Anglo Saxon race holds the balance of power in international affairs and from this time on may be expected to show a united front in dealing with other nations.

§

There is also a reference to the first white child born in Dawson.

"Dear Little Nugget*"*

THE KLONDIKE NUGGET	June, 1898
Gone to Seattle
The first white child born in Dawson, Dawsy Schultz, has left for the outside. The mother, during the entire winter, has been very sick and it has only been within the past month that she has been able to get around at all, so it was thought best by Mr. Schultz to send mother and child outside, he staying in during the coming winter to work in the mines.

§

One police court story dealt at some length with the actions of Mr. Taniguchi whose problems appeared to stem entirely from his racial origin and the story even stated that his daughter was very pretty "from a Japanese point of view."

THE KLONDIKE NUGGET	August, 1898
Court News
R. Taniguchi, a Japanese fellow of low character and complicated disposition, was Monday on complaint of George L. Kershaw, another Jap, charged with the heinous offence of forcing his little daughter, Kumi, to prostitution and living upon her earnings.

The girl looks to be no more than 12 years old with long raven black hair and undoubtedly extremely pretty from a Japanese point of view; she is about 15 and has been an inmate of a brothel in Dawson for over a year. It was upon her request that the complaint was made.

§

In a later edition:

THE KLONDIKE NUGGET	August, 1898

R. Taniguchi, a Japanese gentleman of Oriental ideas and an aversion to work, was fined $50 and given one month in jail. It was first sought to show that he was responsible for the presence of little Kumi in a bagnio and that he was her guardian, but this fell for want of proof and the charge against him was changed to vagrancy which was easy to verify.

§

STROLLER WHITE

News from Dawson's court house was read avidly by *Nugget* subscribers and much of this was written by Elmer J. White, born in Ohio in 1859. White was better known to several decades of newspaper readers in a variety of publications as "Stroller" White. He was an itinerant reporter who found his way to Dawson during the *Nugget*'s brief glory days, but unlike many of his ilk, who wandered in and out of the North, Stroller stayed. Not only did he wind up working for several papers but he also owned some. White then went into politics. He was a Democrat in the Alaska Territorial Legislature in 1918 and later was Speaker of the House.

Most reporters of the day remained largely anonymous. "By-lines" were not used in the *Nugget*, but Stroller became well known through his column. He had a free-flowing style and seldom used one word if he could work in three or four. He was not much interested in serious matters of the day in Dawson: the politics and the battles over claims and properties or the other machinations of the Gold Commissioner's office. Stroller preferred chronicling the daily lives and trials — in court and out — of what he called the flotsam and jetsam of society — the many colourful people who patronized the saloons, dance halls, theatres, gambling tables and red-light districts of Dawson.

Alcohol and prostitution were the two major social problems in the town, so Stroller had lots to write about. He had a slightly jaundiced view of authority and his sympathies generally lay with those down on their luck and those caught up in the often wild, rags to riches, glamorous to tawdry lifestyle that they couldn't handle. He didn't lecture on the evils of alcohol but he liked nothing better than reporting on the characters and the sometimes funny, sometimes sad, stories that unfolded in the court house. He wrote in the tenor of the times, but with sympathy and perception. The underdog always got the break.

While the story has been told in various forms over the years and embellished in many different ways, there is no doubt that the world owes Stroller White recognition for the discovery of ice worms, now part of the great mythology of the North. According to most accounts, Stroller was slightly stuck for a good yarn for the *Nugget*, which was unusual. It was a very chilly winter's day and he was trudging from saloon to saloon when he became aware of the squeaking sound made by the runners of a sled as it slid over the snow. He had an inspiration.

Stroller went back to his office and pecked out a story stating that because of Dawson's extremely cold weather, ice worms in their millions had come up out of the glaciers surrounding Dawson to enjoy the awful freeze. They were chirping happily, so happily in fact that it was keeping people awake at night and something would have to be done about it if the temperature didn't go up and the worms return to the glaciers. *Nugget* readers read it and laughed.

Next day, in the Northern Saloon, they were featuring "Ice Worm Cocktail $1." Stroller ordered one and the crowd watched in amusement. The bartender had lots of worms — small objects embedded in the ice. He broke the ice, took one out with silver tongs, dropped it into a drink and passed it to Stroller. He drank it carefully and announced to the crowd that it was possibly the best worm cocktail it had been his pleasure to enjoy. Everybody agreed that those little pieces of spaghetti certainly looked like ice worms if there were such things as ice worms.

Amazingly, Stroller's simple little yarn picked up a following when it went later to the outside world. A scientific body in London, England, and the U.S. Department of Agriculture were among the groups which asked for more information on this northern phenomenon, but eventually the penny dropped.

Stroller was one of the North's most colourful reporters, a man who took an interest in many things. He died in Juneau, Alaska, in 1930.

The following comments about the French Kid and from a court news column which appeared in the *Nugget* were his work and from the style, it is fairly certain that one item recounting a Police Raid and the tale about Constable Lindbladt and Pauline Densmore also were his. These were his kind of people: "The 'French Kid' registered a win of $1,000 against two banks Friday night. During the subsequent 24 hours, he and his friends enjoyed a hot old time. They stacked chips so high on the layout that the dealers cut them down. They played with the dance hall girls against 'ala mains left' and drank whiskey enough to float the Reindeer. By 7 p.m. Saturday night the Kid had become so helpless he was incapable of rolling a cigaret. His furious time had collapsed by Wednesday. He succeeded in grapevining his way to a chair near an unused card table in the Dominion and then passed into a state of innocuous desuetude."

From Stroller's Court News column comes the following information: "The monotonous grind of the courthouse was relieved Tuesday by the trial of John O'Hara. The prisoner was accused of assaulting his wife, Eva Emma O'Hara, more generally known as Eva St. Clair. The offence was committed on the second floor of the Monte Carlo. With tears glistening in her eyes, Eva recounted the facts related to the violent act of her liege lord; how he struck her for her money and how he tried to separate her from her 'good stuff', and then struck her again but this time over her left optic. All the other witnesses contradicted the fair Eva. Miss Louise Lily Carter, a comely damsel, gushingly informed the magistrate that she saw the whole fracas and that no blows were struck. Robert Winkley testified in corroboration. Then there was 'ze Count de Rouleux' with his hair geometrically pointed down the back of his head to a point in the vicinity of his vertebrae. The Count described that he 'russel ze beer in zee show house box'. He witnessed the whole dispute and swore no assault was attempted. The defendant was an employee of the theatre. He denied having struck his wife and attributed her black eye to the possible fact that in caressing and loving her he might have pressed her left orb too hard against a door jam. The magistrate concluded that Eva was more truthful than the balance of the witnesses for he sentenced her husband to 30 days where there are no ladies left to caress but where the whole system of the universe seems to be interested solely in perpetuating the government fuel supply."

The prose of Stroller White and the vernacular of the community predominates in this comment from the *Nugget*. "On last Saturday the police occasioned quite a flutter among the soiled doves of the tenderloin district. Without warning and at an unusual hour the conservators of propriety awakened the inmates of the various cribs. The girls in dishabille, with disheveled hair and bleary eyes, opened their respective doors expecting to greet a late caller. They were confounded at the sight of the uniformed officers. The purpose of the raid was to apprehend those individuals known as 'macques' in the lower levels of society. Five were arrested, charged with living off the avails. One was sentenced to 30 days at hard labor without the option of a fine. The others go on trial."

Stroller's sense of humour is evident in these comments about one member of the Northwest Mounted Police. It ran under the headline: Const. Lindbladt and Pauline Densmore, Arrested for Creating a Disturbance: "On the way down Pauline tried to win her captor by other tactics. She wheedled and she coaxed. She wept and she pleaded. She had hysterics and she fainted. But there was no wavering in the steady tramp, tramp of Lindbladt and his aides. She became merry. She became affectionate. She suddenly observed the masculine proportions of her captor. He was large and lovable. She yearned to impress. His hands were busy and now how could he resist? She began osculating. She must kiss - and she did. Lindbladt blushed like a boy but proved unyielding and Pauline came to her senses amidst the unusual masculine surroundings of the barracks."

Stroller's Court News was a popular feature even after Gene Allen turned the paper over to his brother and in fact it appeared until the *Nugget*'s final edition. There were few violent crimes and a large number of charges related to over-indulgence. This was the meat for his column. Subscribers read him avidly.

THE KLONDIKE NUGGET   August, 1902
Court News

At 25 cents a drink, a Monte Cristo Hill miner deprived himself of 24 drinks by endeavoring to take more than his share at one session and succeeding in his endeavor. He came to town yesterday rejoicing in strength and vigor, the birds sang, the marigolds blossomed in his heart and life to him had a yellow jasmine hue. But Canadian Club, Seagrams, Haig and Haig and home grown Velvet Tom chased each other down his larynx and by this morning, where hours before birds sang among summer flowers, frogs were croaking amidst the slimy leaves of skunk cabbage and a dark brown taste that causes men to get up at 4 o'clock and drink with relief, water that is alive with wiggletails, pervaded his mouth. A fine of $1 and costs, in all $6, the price of 24 drinks was imposed. Moral — put a little lemon in it.

In the police court Saturday morning, Kittie Howard was committed to jail for 30 days to give her an opportunity to recover from the effects of a protracted spree. She pleaded guilty to the charge of creating a disturbance in the Standard Theatre. As she had not fully recovered from the effects Saturday, as a kindness to her the magistrate ordered her committed for the period mentioned because he had concluded from the information that she would be in the same condition before Monday had she merely been fined and let go.

George Corbut, a Jap, was fined $2 and costs for riding his bike on the sidewalk, and many persons, not Japs, will do well to profit from the penalty imposed on him.

§

THE FLAVOUR OF DAWSON

Life in Dawson in the summer of 1898 had a flavour all its own. These are some of the events which *Nugget* reporters covered and some of the people who became famous in Dawson, for a moment, or for a little longer.

THE KLONDIKE NUGGET   July, 1898
Panning
A crowd of newcomers was gathered in front of the Northern Saloon on Sunday watching the antics of some boys. They were busily engaged in gathering into boxes the swept out sawdust and rubbish from the saloon and had already panned seven dollars in gold dust.

§

THE KLONDIKE NUGGET   July, 1898
Prices
R. G. Gandolfo, a pioneer in nearly every placer or quartz mining camp in the country, and who arrived on the 19th with 16,000 pounds of candies, oranges, lemons, etc., brought the first bananas, cucumbers and ripe tomatoes to Dawson. The bananas brought $1 and the cucumbers $5 each, and at $5 a pound the tomatoes were snapped up

as soon as placed on sale. At wholesale the oranges brought $60 and the lemons $73 per box.

§

J. Morrow Walsh, Commissioner of the Yukon, said he had ordered Mounties to clear obstructions from Front Street.

THE KLONDIKE NUGGET   July, 1898
Clean Up
Campers occupying the streets and private property must move their tents elsewhere. At present the streets are blocked, private property is interfered with and the sanitary condition of the town is threatened. Campers can secure squatters' space on the platform above Dawson at the upper end of Bonanza trail.

§

THE KLONDIKE NUGGET   July, 1898
People
The only point at which tab is kept on the newcomers to the Yukon is at Tagish Post. On June 19, the official register showed that 3,850 boats of all kinds had cleared from there, containing 11,374 men and 240 women. At that date there were another thousand boats in sight.

§

THE KLONDIKE NUGGET   July, 1898
First Cow
The first milk cow ever in Dawson arrived on Wednesday. She was not very well pleased with her surroundings and did not give much milk; but that first milking brought just $30 in Klondike gold dust. She will be treated to the best that Dawson affords — flour and packing case hay. One hundred dollars a milking is not too much to expect of her as she comes from good family and will not do anything to make her ancestors turn over in their graves — more properly speaking, in the stomachs of their patrons. H. L. Miller is the man who brought her in along with 19 male companions. All hail to you, Mrs. Bovine. May your shadow never grow less and may your society improve the people — internally, at least. Welcome you are and it is trusted that your

welcome will bring a stampede of your kind, for it is considered you are a valuable addition to Dawson.

§

A young mine owner, Abraham Gordon, after four years in the Yukon went outside and the *Nugget* reported his experiences.

THE KLONDIKE NUGGET   July, 1898
Young Love
On his return this spring over the trail he found a lady named Mrs. Berrell and her buxom daughter, who were daring the terrors of the pass in order to reach this land of gold. Of course, they had to be helped over bad places and encouraged over dangerous ones, and also, of course, Miss Minnie, being the younger, needed the most encouragement; and who more able to wisely advise and encourage as our gallant Alaskan who had been over the route and knew every menacing rock and rapid? But cupid is a cunning little imp and delights in the roar of canyon or cascade just as much as the perfumed flower gardens of milder climes. And so at the Episcopalian Church, the two became one.

§

The gambling fraternity was talking about the exploits of one man and this was a place where the stakes were high.

THE KLONDIKE NUGGET   July, 1898
Lucky Walter
Walter Leroy, a Texan, tried to locate a mine and could not. He then tried to find employment and failed. Walter, however, with his powerful Texas spirit knew something that he could do. So he straightaway got very drunk. It was not your regular oldtime Texas bender. When he started out, Walter had about $30 or so, and when he woke up next day in the tent of some friends, imagine his surprise to find every pocket bulging with money and his gold pouch so heavy he could hardly carry it. During the night, he had virtually cleaned up every game he struck and when he finally went under the table his friends carried him home, richer than he ever was before or probably will ever be again.

§

DANGEROUS AND DEADLY

The dream of most of the mining rookies on the trail of '98 was to make a fast, easy strike and then get out with a sack full of gold. Few realized they faced tough, back-breaking work or that narrow shafts dug by hand through cement-hard permafrost could be dangerous and deadly. They didn't know about the gas that develops underground in a confined working space lit only by a guttering lamp.

The *Nugget* told of the hardships and the toll exacted at the claims on the creeks. In July, 1898, it told of the fortunate break for one man who could have lost his life digging at Sulphur Stream, where they were getting as much as eight dollars a pan.

THE KLONDIKE NUGGET   July, 1898

Narrow Escape

On claim 17 a workman named Harris was raised to the surface one day last week apparently dead. He had been in the drift some time when he found himself being overcome. Harris had just time to pass a rope around his body and signal the hoister when he was overcome and becoming unconscious. He was hoisted to the surface immediately, yet it was a half day before he could recover.

§

Another man wasn't so lucky. Despite the heroism of his partner, he died alone at the bottom of his shaft. This was at Bonanza, probably a very rich claim.

THE KLONDIKE NUGGET   July, 1898
Prospector Killed
James Shotwell, who owned a half share in bench claim No. 24 on Bonanza, is the last man to fall victim to the fatal gas which has claimed so many lives. He and his partner had a shaft down 110 feet and he on Friday last went down to place a fire. Later in the afternoon the fire had gone out and Shotwell went down to replace it. At the bottom he called to the other men to hoist him. When he was unable to hold the rope his partner immediately started down but he was unable to proceed but a short distance before he was forced back. Shotwell's body later was recovered.

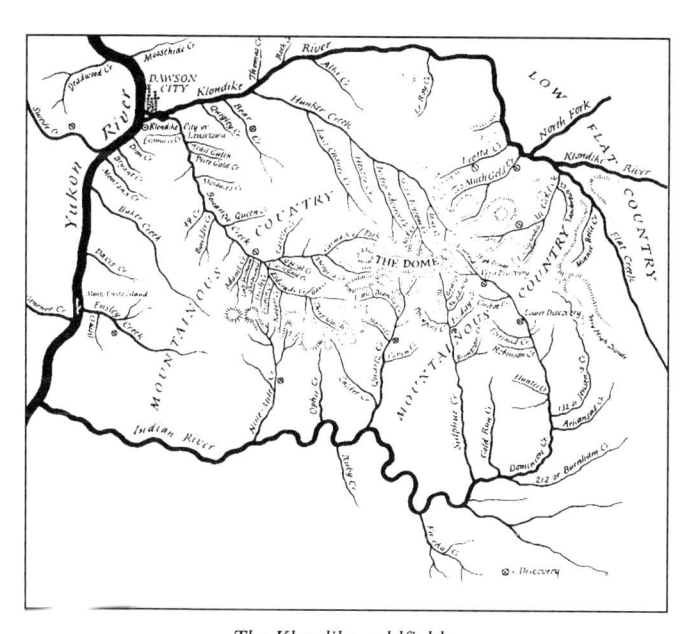

§

The Klondike goldfields.

How the World Saw It

The Klondike gold rush, from the moment the first ships arrived in San Francisco and Seattle carrying tons of gold and the newly rich, captured the world's imagination, and reporters and writers quickly made it one of the most extensively covered events of the 19th century. It was relatively easy for correspondents to reach the Klondike, unburdened by the equipment and provisions carried by would-be prospectors.

The event also came at the end of a North American depression and at a time of economic stagnation in much of Europe. Tales of the great wealth to be easily attained and the ease with which nuggets could be plucked from the ground blossomed with the first reports. They were, however, fairly quickly dispelled by some straight writing about the hardships to be endured and the odds against getting rich quick.[3]

Some of the gaudiest tales came from writers who never actually got to the Klondike. *The New York Journal* had a fanciful yarn which stated, "There abound reminiscences of the slaughter of innumerable bands of early colonists and explorers...." Before the gold rush there were few people in the Yukon other than native Indians and some prospectors, and most certainly no "innumerable banks of early colonists and explorers...." to be slaughtered.

Major news operations rushed in teams of reporters. They represented William Randolph Hearst, *Reuters, The Manchester Guardian, The Times of London, The Toronto Globe*, and even *Le Temps* of Paris.

The *Guardian*'s A.N.C. Treadgold summed it up best, stating that the Klondike had become "... a newspaper property and the newspaper correspondents have not, as a whole been possessed of the qualifications of mind and body needed by those who desire to convey information about so important a gold field as the Klondike. The Klondike country ... is so difficult for the ordinary traveller that it is small wonder if newspaper correspondents as a whole have sat still at Dawson or even further away and retailed second-hand information gathered from sources, at best, unreliable."

Treadgold marvelled at the law and order in Dawson. Saloons there were aplenty but governed by law "... and to see them close at twelve on Saturday and for a whole Sunday's rest is a sight to make a man think." He also wrote: "The main street is nearly always crowded with men trying to find one another .... When you find your man the two of you sit on the edge of the sidewalk (raised a foot above the road for cleanliness) and talk. This is a picturesque sight, to see men of all nations, in all kinds of quaint garments, standing or sitting at business in the main street."

On Sundays the strains of old familiar hymns could be heard, and he wrote that for a little while some did not feel so far from home after all.

The main street was far from clean and far from quiet. The Reuters correspondent noted: "The main street of Dawson is supposed to be a business thoroughfare, but from end to end it is an almost unbroken succession of saloons, dance halls and gambling dens. The saloons dispense the most pernicious kind of poison, which they have the affrontery to call 'whiskey' at 50 cents a thimbleful without the necessity of contributing in any way towards the expense of governing the country."

Flora Shaw, the colonial editor for *The Times of London*, was one of the few women reporters in Dawson. She described the main street as "nothing more than a land of alternate bog-holes stretching for about a mile and dust-heaps with saloons and sawmills, warehouses and wharves." She raised a storm when she blasted living conditions in the city, railing at the disparities of great wealth and poverty. She also thought that the local laws were bad and the officials not only corrupt but irresponsible and negligent.

Shaw wrote: "The unsanitary condition of Dawson, situated as the town is upon a swamp and devoid of the most elementary provisions for cleanliness and health, is a standing menace to the community. Typhoid is permanently in the town; the death rate is abnormally high; and there are as yet no signs of any measures to be taken to avert the danger of a serious outbreak of the epidemic."

She toned down her views later, but it is possible her criticism helped stir local officials into action. While there continued to be much sickness, Dawson was spared the ravages of a full-blown epidemic.

Faith Fenton, her hat always jammed on her head and her skirt sweeping the ground, told Toronto's *Globe* readers of the thousands of men crowding Dawson's streets, many with apparently no intention of going after gold but with a desire to get out and get home. With winter fast approaching in 1898, Fenton wrote: "Think of it. A city of 16,000 souls, and the centre of a district of 30,000, a live busy city, with its streets thronged with men, its busy warehouses, its growing interests and civic problems, shut away entirely three months in the year." She was one who stayed. In 1900 she married the Yukon's medical health officer and made her home in Dawson for several years.

Julius Price wrote a 12-part series for *The Illustrated London News* entitled, "From Euston to the Klondike." He described Dawson when he arrived just after the main flotilla: "Try and picture to yourself a wide flat stretch of marshy ground, with a background of high hill, on the shore of a mighty river rushing swiftly by: and cover this shore with as many tents of all shapes and sizes as your imagination can picture. In the water and along the beach facing these tents place hundreds of the roughest wooden boats and of all imaginable builds, some afloat, others drawn up on the shingle. Then draw further on your imagination and see a big motley crowd of men and women and children, in all sorts and conditions of garb, round and about the tents, boats and everywhere; and above all a blazing sun, and plenty of dust blown about by a persistent wind, - and you have Dawson, the golden city, as it appeared to me as I landed on the 14th of June, 1898."

Another writer found that the Gold Commissioner's office was totally corrupt and "Dawson represented the British system at its worst ... a superficial officialdom stifling all enterprise."

THE GOLD COMMISSIONER

Without doubt, Dawson's Gold Commissioner, Thomas Fawcett, had an unenviable reputation. Said one editorial in the *Nugget* in August, 1898: "Was ever such a policy of intolerable vacillation before forced upon an unsuspicious and confiding people? Was ever there such a travesty on impartial administration? Did ever men of our race before submit in silence to such outrageous impositions as are daily being forced upon them?"

When Allen arrived in Dawson there already was much unhappiness over the administration of the only thing that really mattered, the finding and mining of gold.

The mostly American miners felt there was too much British-style red tape and regulation, but what they really objected to was the imposition of royalties, a ten-per-cent tax on all gold taken from the ground after the initial $2,500 was removed. Later it was estimated that the government collected much less than it should have, much gold being quietly shipped out of the Yukon without the payment of taxes. But gold was all that mattered in Dawson, colouring every happening and every move, and Allen knew a popular cause when he saw one. He moved quickly to become the miners' friend, including sending a delegation to Ottawa with their complaints.

Fawcett was a bit of a stuffed shirt, and possibly not the most competent offical in the gold-mining town, but the job would have daunted the most brilliant. There was chaos and confusion surrounding all aspects of the stampede. There were fights and squabbles over staking and claims, many of those scouring the creeks knowing next to nothing about prospecting.

It was acknowledged by many observers that without doubt there was corruption in the commissioner's office. The staff, handling business in the millions, was woefully underpaid. Some miners' claims were disputed and on so-called legal grounds, invalidated, while others seemingly in the know moved in. Some areas were temporarily closed to staking, but when the time for opening arrived, it was clear that some stampeders had had inside information and had moved in ahead of the rest.

The *Nugget*'s fight was backed up by comments from Yukon Commissioner James Walsh in an interview about insider knowledge on staking at Dominion Creek.

THE KLONDIKE NUGGET   September, 1898
Editorial

Major Walsh says he is sick of the whole business. His exact words are: "The administration of affairs on Dominion Creek has been a mess from start to finish and I am sick and tired of the whole business."

Good for Major Walsh. He has practically admitted that which the people have known for lo these many days, viz: That the Gold Commissioner is incompetent to fill the office that he now holds.

Be he ever so honest himself, the Gold Commissioner's office has been conducted in such a manner as to give evidence of much crooked work. Information that the public should have, as soon as anybody, has been given out on the quiet by someone to friends, and those friends have taken the information thus surreptitiously gained and located for themselves that which has been denied the honest prospector.

§

Walsh's words had pretty well cooked Fawcett's goose and the *Nugget* returned again and again to the battle and to the charge that he must go. Allen endeared himself to the men of the creeks. *Nugget* sales soared and the headlines told of victory.

THE KLONDIKE NUGGET   November, 1898
Goodbye Fawcett
A British Columbian to Take His Position
Congratulations to the Miners of the Klondike are in Order

§

When the new commissioner arrived the next month, the *Nugget* blew its own horn and the headlines read:

THE KLONDIKE NUGGET   December, 1898
It Has Been Given to the Jury
Case of the People Vs Incompetent Public Officials
The Verdict Sustains the Nugget in its Fight
Public Opinion Brings to a Long Suffering People, a Change of Officials

§

In all of this Allen and his scrappy *Nugget* had been the judge and jury. Its readers were happy.

HOT DUSTY SUMMER

By July, 1898, summer heat had settled on the dusty, crowded streets of the burgeoning town. People were still arriving and hopes were high in the hearts of the newcomers. They scanned the pages of the *Nugget* for the latest news and gossip. The paper told them of the joys and the price of melons, the dreaded barbers' itch and other happenings as the summer wore on, including the creation of the Yukon as a territory distinct from the Northwest Territories.

THE KLONDIKE NUGGET   July, 1898

Cheap at the Price

Water melon from the warm and sunny south — south of here anyhow — are for sale in Dawson. Think of measly 10 cent water melon, carried a couple of thousand miles, shaken up and then offered for sale. In the U.S., the land of water melons, the melon would be prosecuted as a public health nuisance, a threat to the general health. Not so in Dawson, $25 in good Eldorado dust was paid for that water melon by some one to whom green curves evoked the recollection of days when nuggets were not too plentiful but water melons were.

§

THE KLONDIKE NUGGET   July, 1898
                         The Itch
   One of the most disagreeable, aggravating diseases to affect a man's beard, which is very prevalent in Dawson, is known as barbers' itch. It is a skin disease causing large blotches upon the shaven portion of the face, painful to the victim and annoying to the eye. Several of our citizens are affected by it. It is caused by the use of unclean cups, dirty shaving brushes, and the use of soiled towels in barbers' shops. For this there is hardly any excuse as water is abundant in Dawson.
   With shaving and haircuts at prices of 50 cents and a dollar and upwards, the public might at least have commensurate service. This loathsome disease can be avoided by the use of one's own razor and equipment at home. A little blade scrape with a keen blade is better than the looks and the effects of the barber's itch.

§

August, 1898, brought an announcement in the *Nugget* of the change in status for the community which was now part of the Yukon. In fact it had been part of the Yukon since May but it took three months for the news to reach Dawson.

THE KLONDIKE NUGGET   August, 1898
              We Are Now The Yukon Territory
   An Act of May 27, Separated us from the Balance of the Northwest
           A Commissioner and Six Others Form a Council
           A Majority of the Body Will Constitute a Quorum

§

This court news column could have been written by Stroller White, but was probably done by a predecessor.

THE KLONDIKE NUGGET   August, 1898
                        Court News
   Mrs. E. Chronister was a disturber of our quiet little neighboring burg of Klondike City, and Klondike City "hooch" is not good for staid matrons of the "klootch" persuasion as was demonstrated by certain unladylike language. It was a long way to bring her over so it took $50 and costs to get her back.

   The past four days have been busy as usual. The most important item to chronicle is that a Klondike standard of prices has been adopted in the case of "common drunks." Instead of $5 the price is now to be $20 which is only in proportion to the improved quality of the whiskey since the ice went out.

Charles Williamson got six months hard labor for playing a naughty prank on the Northern. He tried to blow a sack of clay pretending it was gold. The trick was discovered and Charles now languishes in jail.

Gussie Bolden and Eva Dewar were mulcted of the sum of $59 and costs. Their offence was of the kind described as "ladies of easy virtue."

Alice Lanesville, Lillie Gilmour and Eva Durant were fined $50 and costs each for "indecent and shameless acts at the Nidga." Complaints had been received from time to time but no one was willing to appear as a witness for the prosecution. A detachment of police in civilian dress was ordered to the scene and long terms of imprisonment await the three if the thing is repeated.

§

In the same edition, the *Nugget* told of the travails of a wandering harpist who played at the Nidga. It is assumed he also got nicked by the plain-clothes police:

THE KLONDIKE NUGGET   August, 1898
Harpist Fined
G. E. Gustave Arconti, an Italian harp player, was fined $25 and costs for not knowing the character of the people in the Nidga when they hired him.

§

THE KLONDIKE NUGGET   August, 1898
Advertisement
Marie Riedeselle
Leading Professional Masseuse
From 121 West 111th Street, New York City
Elegant Parlors on Second Avenue, Four Doors
North of Pioneer Drug Store, Dawson City
Gives Massage, Russian, Turkish
Medicated and Plain Baths
Rheumatism Successfully Treated

Scurvy Prevented and Cured by New Method
Lost Vitality Restored
Also Facial Specialist
Special attention given to Treatment of the Scalp, Removal of Dandruff, Prevention of Hair Falling Out and Restoring Same to its Natural Growth.
Note - Special Comfortable Room for a Patient Who Would Prefer Home Comfort to Hospital Treatment.

§

While prices in Dawson were astronomically high compared to other communities, the late summer of 1898 brought bargains to the community for the first time, the result of many broken dreams and a recognition by some that it was time to get out before winter returned.

THE KLONDIKE NUGGET   August, 1898

Trading

Petticoat Lane in London does not allow any more active trading or greater slashing of prices on clothing than can be found on Dawson

Dawson City in summer, after the steamers were able to ascend the Yukon River (COURTESY SPECIAL COLLECTIONS DIVISION, UNIVERSITY OF WASHINGTON LIBRARIES, PHOTO BY WEBSTER & STEVENS, NEGATIVE 56A,#2.)

sandbar today. Many people want to get out before winter. The sandbar has been laid out into two principal streets — Wall Street and Bowery Ave. Many people want to sell at 50 per cent the price of clothing in Seattle or Victoria.

Some goods at auction - oak sled a dollar; suits of oilskins a dollar and a half; tents from two and a half; boots, shoes, rubber boots and the thousand and one things we all brought with us going at prices that would make a Clark St., Chicago, second-hand man sick with envy. Everything must be sold and quickly.

What bitter disappointments some of these people will have to recount when they get outside. At Sheep Camp, with the trip barely commenced, better prices would have been obtained for everything, yet they lugged and tugged, packed-up over snow and over hills of ice, faced storms and dangerous rivers, took their lives in their hands hundreds of times, many of them dying from overwork and the result of exposure. It isn't at all surprising that there are long faces among them this summer. The nights are getting darker and this betokens the approach of winter and the light heartedness and the levity notable on the trail has flown.

§

The threat of fire always was something to be feared in Dawson, but there was the odd outbreak with its humorous side. Such was the case with "Belle's Blaze."

THE KLONDIKE NUGGET   September, 1898
Belle's Blaze
About 5 a.m. Thursday, fire destroyed the "Welcome", a sumptuously furnished cabin on Third occupied by Belle Mitchell and the girl known as Tony.

There being no fire department in town, there was no organized effort to subdue the flames, though plenty of men stood about ready to do all in their power. Charlie Kimball had a pail of spring water in his place a few doors away and donated it to the good cause. He also had a barrel of vinegar handy and hurriedly stoved in the head and proceeded to use the contents on the fierce flames. However, just at this time someone happened to think there was plenty of swamp water in the ditch in front of the burning building. This is, probably, what saved Charlie's whiskey, for he might next have devoted that precious scurvy-curing liquid to the quenching of the roaring flames.

A man arrived after flames died down and started panning the ashes, working towards the pay streak under the burned gold scales. Belle Mitchell observed him and gave him such a stinging slap on the side of the head that he hurriedly dropped his gold pan and sought the dreary solitude of his own cogitations in private.

§

THE KLONDIKE NUGGET   September, 1898
Dawson Needs a Public School
There are enough children in Dawson to warrant a good sized building. The private schools should be encouraged by every possible means. But we hold the opinion that the community at large owes it to itself to see that every child who desires to attend school should be given an opportunity to do so without charge.

§

THE KLONDIKE NUGGET   September, 1898
Winter's on the Way
The population is thinning down rapidly to its winter dimensions. The creeks are filling up and streams deserted for the summer are beginning to teem with tireless miners. A week or two more will see sufficient snow to allow the sledding of provisions to the various claims.

The merchants of the city are bolstering their winter preparation and at the present time there are 227 buildings in the process of construction.

The majority of the population came here with a year's outfit and little intention of remaining much longer and many could not find it in their hearts to stay even that long.

§

Princess of the Yukon

Little Margie Newman was called the "Princess of the Yukon" and briefly, at nine years of age, was one of the brightest stars on the Klondike stage in the summer of '98. Her brothers, Willie and George, hoofed and sang in the family act, but it was Margie who tugged at the hearts of lonely men far from home and many threw nuggets onto the stage when she appeared.

One even wrote a poem which began: "God Bless you, Little Margie, for you made us better men; God Bless you Little Margie, for you take us home again."

The *Nugget* reported her appearance at a Sunday night charity benefit for hospitals in the Oatley Sisters theatre.

THE KLONDIKE NUGGET   October, 1898
Princess Performs

Little nine-year-old Margie Newman is probably the sweetest and as clever a child as it has ever been our pleasure to listen to and watch on the stage. She appears sometimes with her brothers, and they are both clever boys, but there is a natty newness and conscientiousness about the girl that has endeared her to the hearts of the men who go so often to see her. Some of her songs have been heard in Dawson before but the old rounders to a man declare that they have never been sung before with such pleasure to the audience or to the positive improvement of the song. "To your health, Margie."

§

Margie knocked them cold at another benefit with her version of "Annie Laurie."

THE KLONDIKE NUGGET   October, 1898
Margie Sings Annie Laurie
The little favorite was in Scottish costume and sang Annie Laurie. She also responded with the highland fling. It is a wonder Margie is not spoiled by the amount of adulation she generally receives for with the little lady at the governor's right hand, the seat of honor, Colonel Day arose and proposed the only toast of the evening. "To little Margie, The Princess of the Yukon, and dearest to the hearts of every man, woman and child in the Yukon." The toast was drunk and with much enthusiasm. Most children would have been confused with the attention of so many gentlemen, but when the governor lifted her onto the table to respond, she said, "Ladies and Gentlemen, I didn't come to make a speech but I thank every one of you."

§

Willie and George also performed, but, as always, they got barely a mention. Later, as though Margie hadn't picked up enough money for the Newman family, there was a benefit staged at the Monte Carlo and the *Nugget* recorded:

THE KLONDIKE NUGGET   November, 1898
Friends Honour Margie Newman
At the close of her number, Captain Jack carried the little princess on the stage in his arms, made a pretty little presentation speech and pinned to her dress a beautiful gold brooch presented to her by admiring friends, while coins of all denominations, nuggets and boxes of candy rained on the stage from admirers in the auditorium.

§

Like the gold rush itself, little Margie's fame was fleeting. The family left the Klondike and came back to Dawson a few years later. But the magic was gone, along with most of the people and money, and little Margie was just another singer.

Fire

The ever-present possibility that a wall of fire could roar through Dawson's jam-packed log and frame buildings was a threat that worried many, but arguments about who should pay for protection caused dithering and delays. Downtown Dawson was a tinderbox, a disaster waiting to happen. Building regulations barely existed and were largely ignored. Heating often was a crude wood stove with a white-hot pipe reaching up through the ceiling. Oil lamps provided light and there were lots of careless smokers. A water supply to fight any blaze was a problem in the winter when the river was frozen.

It was ironic that when the police bugle sounded the alarm on October 24, 1898, some fire-fighting equipment had arrived in town. A debate raged, however, about who would pay for it and no effort had been made to secure trained crews to man it. For hours the fate of Dawson was in doubt. An army of miners and others fought to make fire breaks and stop the advance of the flames as they quickly ate up the bone-dry buildings and shacks.

While some were prepared to risk their lives, there were others who jealously guarded their water pails and didn't want to give them to the bucket brigade that was frantically scooping water from the river. The desperate situation also fortunately found men in town with fire-fighting expertise and know-how. They started to use the unpaid-for equipment that was lying outside a warehouse. There were axes, hooks, ladders and an engine. Charlie Bush, a former assistant fire chief in Victoria, was prominent in pulling together the volunteers.

As the *Nugget* reported: "Paint and tallow were hastily scraped from the steam engine's bearings and in two hours the engine was down to the edge of the river on Second Street with hose stretched to the scene of the fire. However, the boys with the axes, ropes, pails and hooks had confined the fire before water could be put in the boiler and steam raised."

The steam from the fire engine was, nonetheless, greeted with a cheer, for then and not until then was the town known to be safe. This is what the *Nugget* told its readers:

THE KLONDIKE NUGGET   October 15, 1898
Front Street Fire

The air was cold and frosty and the inhabitants of closely built Front Street were yet for the greater part wrapped in slumber when in the rear upper rooms of the Green Tree Saloon and Hotel the flames were first perceived breaking from the windows in roaring force.

People rushed to help remove mail from the adjoining post office, which was reduced to ashes in 20 minutes. People scrambled out of the handsome Worden Hotel before it was engulfed.

Distracted people scampered in every direction with gigantic loads of household valuables and teams commenced hurriedly to arrive and were quickly drafted into service.

Gigantic efforts were made to organize bucket brigades but for a long time people were slow to work for the public good.

Second-hand dealers were strong armed into turning over any buckets they had. Before too long, three lines of men were passing water from the river, but nevertheless the wind carried an immense volume of flames across Front Street and in an instant the shell buildings on the waterfront were also in flames.

Quickly engulfed were a bakery, a jewelers, the New England Saloon, the Vancouver Hotel and its 10 cabins, and 16 waterfront buildings. Miners working the creeks saw the smoke in the sky, knew the dangers if Dawson was totally destroyed with winter on the way, and many hurried to help.

§

It was finally realized that the town could only be saved if breaks were created by demolishing buildings in the fire's path. Ropes were attached to the corners of log cabins and then with a long, strong pull they were torn down log by log. Frame buildings were hewed and chopped into kindling wood. At least 2,000 men fought the fire.

The *Nugget* said some of the best work was done at times with a tin cup and an occasional pail of precious water and one reporter commented: "Scorched buildings surround the burning district and everyone was saved by the persistent and fearless efforts of the citizens, police and military. Men stayed on buildings and on roofs until their clothes scorched their skin in their determined fight against further encroachment of the flames."

After the smoke had cleared it was estimated that loss was in excess of a half-million dollars and probably more when personal effects were considered. There was no insurance in Dawson.

The *Nugget* reported that if the fire equipment had been ready for action, the blaze could have been confined to the Green Tree Saloon and Hotel for the loss of about $20,000. The catastrophe jarred Dawson into action. A finance committee of citizens signed notes for $12,000 to pay for more fire equipment. On October 27, less than two weeks after the blaze, a volunteer fire department was formed and began drilling and training. A chief and an assistant were elected, three captains were appointed and 100 men were on the roll. They were needed.

Six months later, on April 26, 1899, fire again devastated Dawson. Loss this time was in excess of a million dollars with more than 100 buildings going up in smoke and flames.

Fortunately, in neither blaze was there loss of life, but in the second fire, poor Helen Holden was blamed. She lived in a room over the Bodega Saloon. A six-man jury investigating the blaze found no evidence to show how the fire started, but they made this recommendation: "All women-of-the-town be excluded from all public buildings other than licensed hotels."

In the Fall of 1898

Formality was not a major factor of life in the gold-rush days and marriages and marriage ceremonies had a certain free-flowing style. The *Nugget* carried this notice:

THE KLONDIKE NUGGET   September, 1898

Certificate of Marriage. Headquarters of the King of the Klondike. I Siwash George, King of the Klondike, at Dawson, Y.T., do hereby certify that on this 27th day of September, 1898 at 11 p.m. in the City of Dawson, Yukon Territory, Lewis Haber, 24, born in New Orleans and residing in Dawson, and Malamute Annie, aged 19 years, born in Moosehide and now residing in Lousetown, were united in Marriage before me, and in my presence by Bishop Bompas who is authorized by law to perform such a ceremony. Siwash George, King of the Klondike. Per Cupid.

§

Legal? Doubtful, but how about this one performed poetically by French Joe, also known as J. Durant.

THE KLONDIKE NUGGET   October, 1898

Certificate of Marriage
Ten miles from the Yukon on the banks of this lake,
For a partner to Koyukuk McGillis I Take,

> We have no preacher and we have no ring
> It makes no difference it's all the same thing.
>
> Aggie Dalton
>
> I swear by my gee-pole under this tree,
> A devoted husband to Aggie I always will be,
> I'll love and protect her — this maiden so frail —
> From them sourdough stiffs on the Koyukuk Trail.
>
> Frank McGillis
>
> For two dollars apiece in chechako money,
> I unite this couple in matrimony,
> He be a rancher; she be a teacher;
> I do the job up, just as well as a preacher.
>
> French Joe

§

The treatment of animals in Dawson sometimes was little better than it had been on the trail and destitute people were often unable or unwilling to care for their animals.

THE KLONDIKE NUGGET October, 1898

Horse Killed

The peculiar traits of the native dog were clearly demonstrated on Friday night last when a horse owned by George Forman and French Pete was attacked by a band of huskies and literally torn to pieces.

The horse for some reason had become lame and was lying on the ground. In this condition, the huskies found and attacked it. There were about six in the pack and before long the horse was being torn limb from limb. The horse was discovered and its sufferings ended by a bullet.

§

CAD WILSON

There was no doubt that Cad Wilson had been brought at great expense to the Klondike to entertain. A petite redhead, she was no great shakes as a singer or dancer. There were even the ungallant who said she was no great looker, but Cad had a personality that grabbed the miners and the saloon goers of Dawson. Her salty humour was meant for a mining town and the men packed the Tivoli and the Orpheum to hear her. Her wages were matched many times over by the adoring fans who pelted the stage with nuggets and money when she appeared. Some of her richer admirers donated their finest nuggets to make a belt for Cad that went one and a half times around her waist. It is estimated she took about $30,000 from the Yukon in '98 in addition to her nuggets, which included a large one in her garter.

What appealed to the miners, however, didn't sit so well with a more sedate crowd, including some of the city's matrons who showed up one night for a benefit billed as family entertainment. As the *Nugget* recorded it: "Cad Wilson is undoubtedly popular and her repertoire extensive, but there can be no excuse at all for her break with faith with the people who had been assured over and over again that there would be nothing but what a gentleman might take his wife and family to hear and to see with perfect safety to their sense of propriety."

Without going into detail and maintaining all modesty, the *Nugget* explained that for audiences of miners, performers "allow themselves to use what they call 'ginger'." The report said Cad made no new friends for herself with this audience. "Her audacity caused applause in the rear of the hall, but the ladies in front hung their heads and their escorts wished they had never brought them. It was an exhibition of exceedingly bad taste on the part of the performer." It is said many of them left in high dudgeon. It can be assumed that Cad didn't give a damn and the boys at the back had enjoyed the "ginger."

Thanksgiving of a Sort

The great bulk of the people of Dawson were Americans, and for the lonely — and loneliness was the great disease, particularly for those with hopes dashed waiting to get out — November of 1898 was not a good time.

Thanksgiving in the United States is the great holiday of the year, a time of going home to celebrate with family and friends. Few of the men and women of Dawson had families with them and there were no phones on which to call home. The *Nugget* knew this and took a lighter tone in its so-called proclamation issued that November, calling for corned beef at least in the absence of turkey.

THE KLONDIKE NUGGET   November, 1898
A Proclamation

Whereas, the time of year has arrived when all Yankeedom is wont to cease from active toil and pay homage to the shrine of King Turkey and cranberry sauce; and whereas in this remote and far distant neck of the woods, said turkey and sauce are not in evidence to any considerable extent; therefore be it now proclaimed and ordered, and may all loyal lovers of the aforesaid give ear unto this command: That Thursday, the 2nd of November, is here and now set apart as a day of general feasting and rejoicing among the subjects of the star spangled banner, and all dutiful and loving persons do desist from partaking of their wonted cut of beans and bacon, and if unable to secure the requisite turkey are directed to indulge in corned beef or other equally expensive luxury. Done in the year of our Lord, 1898, at 44 degrees below zero.

§

The plight of the destitute at Thanksgiving may have prompted Isaac Lewis to take action, if he concluded that life in the "log house" was preferable to life on the street.

THE KLONDIKE NUGGET   November, 1898
Court News
Isaac Lewis made a sad indiscretion. A man that will "swipe" a tent with the thermometer at 40 below deserves a month in the care of the stripe-legged boys who live in the log house.

§

But all was not doom and gloom in November, 1898, for the *Nugget* also reported some entertaining events.

THE KLONDIKE NUGGET   November, 1898
They Boxed a 10-Round Draw
Wednesday night witnessed the contest between Dick Agnew and the Black Prince at the Monte Carlo Theatre. The affair was pulled off at the conclusion of the regular stage performance and a 20-foot ring was roped off. The boxes, gallery, stage and pit were full of interested spectators. The two men are lightweights and were trained down to fine form. The colored man led his opponent by about four pounds in weight and his form was a model of proportion. Dick stripped rather thin in flesh with good shoulders and chest and arms which outreached his opponent.

§

THE KLONDIKE NUGGET   November, 1898
Rink Flooded
The steam fire engine was given a reliability test last Friday when it was taken over to flood the skating rink for the last time. The thermometer was 40 below zero and the engine stationed upon the river forced a stream with considerable force through 2000 feet of hose without freezing.

§

THE KLONDIKE NUGGET   November, 1898

Advertisement
Tonight at Pioneer Hall
Clean-Cut Family Entertainment
Wondroscope
Moving Pictures of the Spanish-American War
100 Views — Admission — $1

§

THE ALL-CANADIAN ROUTE

To have advocated, as some Canadian officials did, that it was easy to get from Edmonton, Alberta, to Dawson using a poorly defined land and river route was almost criminal. It was more than 1,500 miles across land that was not mapped in detail — rugged land dissected by roaring rapids and spectacular canyons, hills and dense forests. It was rough, dangerous country, passable only by men used to the wilderness and canoeing its waters, and skilled in surviving in a region where the cold could kill and the sun could bake.

Some officials obviously thought that an all-Canadian route to Dawson would be a major coup and that passage through the United States could then be ignored. The merchants in the small community of Edmonton saw a chance to bring in all kinds of supplies and sell them at a sharp markup to the gold seekers. The Klondike rush gave a hefty boost to the local economy and helped Edmonton increase in size and stature.

For those enticed to try the route, it was a different story — one of disappointment, despair, suffering and death. None arrived in Dawson in time to make any kind of killing. In fact, of the thousands who tried the Edmonton route, only a handful ever reached Dawson. Most turned back realizing the trip was hopeless — there were also those who died.

Some were on the move for two years. The *Nugget* told the tale of one man and then gave its assessment of the route.

THE KLONDIKE NUGGET　　　　　　　　　　　November, 1898
Over the All-Canadian Route
14 months from Edmonton to Dawson

Mr. Charles Tobin arrived in Dawson Tuesday after a fearful trip over the All-Canadian route from Edmonton. Mr. Tobin came through with Inspector Wood of the NWMP over the All-Canadian route proposed for them by the government and were 14 months making the trip. The trip as may be expected from the length of time consumed and the route traversed was one of perilous periods of hardship. Men of the party fell sick and turned back until our adventurers were nearly alone. Hudson Bay Company posts were found along the route laid out for them but invariably the stores were found depleted or even deserted. At last Lake Teslin was reached and a boat built and with the aid of provisions picked up in odd lots the weary traveller, Tobin, reached Selkirk a month ago and was frozen in. It is a trip even the most adventurous would not care to duplicate and sufficiently perilous to satisfy the most western appetite. Time and again they were on the verge of starvation and but for the game or fish might have died back in the unsurveyed and untraversed wilderness.

Mr. Tobin is a young man of good physique and good health and possibly in the end will not find himself much injured. Coming down from the Pelly, he froze his nose and face which he doesn't regard as serious. He is the stepson of Mr. A. Powers, Queen's Counsel of the Ottawa Bar.

§

THE KLONDIKE NUGGET　　　　　　　　　　　July, 1899
Trail Tragedies

Stragglers who started for the Yukon via the Edmonton route are still coming in. Many of these men have been on the way for a period of more than 18 months while not a few have been fully two years in their endeavors to reach Dawson. They tell a story of hardships and privation and disasters that almost pass belief.

Some 40 men are still enroute on the Stewart River and fear has been expressed by those who have succeeded in reaching Dawson that many of these unfortunates will find a watery grave in the river which runs for 200 miles and is said to be one continuous succession of canyons and cateracts. They experienced grim tragedy in connection with the stampede to the Klondike, the extent of which will never be fully realized.

§

THE DANCE-HALL GIRLS

The *Nugget* as a general rule loved to vent its wrath on government officials, gouging companies, monopolies and politicians and not necessarily in that order. Conversely, it always had a soft spot for the underdog: the sick and the suffering, the poor and the lonely. It turned out its best purple prose when telling its readers of the tragedies that befell some of the dance-hall girls, young women attracted like moths to a flame by Dawson, the excitement, the glamour as they saw it and the money they thought could be so easily made. Some did make it, most didn't.

Behind the bright lights of the smoky, noisy saloons and dance halls, there was a brittle excitement that could be shattered easily. The girls were young. Many drank too much and hustling drinks was part of their business. They danced with the lonely miners for one dollar a dance and in some halls could work in as many as 80 dances through a long night and into the dawn. They also entertained the patrons in many different ways.

Sometimes sick, sometimes desperate, some were struck by tragedy ... often with a cruel suddenness. The *Nugget* related the stories of three of these girls, two suicides and one murder victim.

Nineteen-year-old Myrtle Brocee was a girl from Ontario who came to Dawson in the summer of '98 to entertain and do whatever else was necessary to make a living. Just before Christmas, Myrtle shot herself

"Dear Little Nugget"

through the head. The *Nugget* fretted about her good name, and vexed over the tough life that so many of the dance-hall girls and would-be entertainers found in Dawson. Myrtle had been ill for three weeks and living in a room above Sam Bonnifield's saloon.

According to the *Nugget*: "By all accounts Myrtle earnestly tried to be a good girl in Dawson, but in that fact lay her unhappiness and undoing. How many will believe this of a variety girl? She was a girl seen drinking wine with men in the boxes and her occupation exposed her to every temptation."

Readers were told that Myrtle and her sister, Florence, formed a song-and-dance act and performed in Canada and the U.S. before learning of the money they could make in "Gold City." They made their way to Dawson and caught on at the Tivoli. But life for them was not all beer and skittles.

As the *Nugget* said: "The standard of virtue for her profession was not set very high. Tempters appeared by the score, some with wine and many of them well off; yet the girl's good name continued, and continued also to make her the more desirable in the eyes of admirers." This was the era when the "Klondike Kings" pelted the stage with nuggets if they liked a particular performer.

Myrtle, it seems, had a liking for wine and instead of wealth she found hardship; instead of honourable suitors she found tempters. The *Nugget* said that while she appeared cheerful most of the time, Myrtle had threatened suicide on several occasions. It asked: "Who can picture the horror which occasionally swallowed the girl's consciousness when she perceived the tentacles of that octupus of fate slowly but surely reaching up to engulf her in its dark hued noisome folds?" Powerful stuff.

She got sick in November and moved in above the saloon where a man named Woolrich offered her his room. Three weeks later she killed herself, using a revolver she had taken from the adjoining room of the attending physician, Dr. Richardson.

At the inquest, her sister, Florence, said she thought Myrtle had been living with Woolrich.

Dr. Richardson said he had not known her to drink much and there was no reason to think she had been recently seduced. Woolrich testified he had shared the room with her during her convalescence, "but she was virtuous all the same."

Florence retained Attorney Sheridan to protect Myrtle from an unqualified verdict of suicide. The jury found she took her life while temporarily insane.

THE KLONDIKE'S

THE KLONDIKE NUGGET   November, 1898
Death of a Dance Hall Girl

The unfortunate girl was laid away as she would have desired had she been a witness to the circumstances. A shapely casket, covered with white cloth; with massive silver-plated handles and trimmings held the remains.

The interior was upholstered with blue and white silk. The dead girl was habited in a beautifully trimmed dress of white satin with needle-worked ruffles. White satin shoes adorned the feet which so often tripped the light fantastic for the amusement of Dawson. The absence of flowers in this land of gloom is painfully apparent. The Rev. Grant read the funeral service where the body had lain in state.

§

Dr. Richardson was one of the pallbearers; Woolrich wasn't. Myrtle was laid to rest in grounds overlooking the Klondike. The *Nugget* continued to worry and late in November printed an editorial which said in part:

THE KLONDIKE NUGGET   November, 1898
Editorial

The statements she was an absolutely good girl, are entitled to credence because it is much more natural for men to boast of a conquest than a failure of purpose. Little was to be lost by their acknowledging intimacy with an actress who was so carelessly throwing her reputation to the winds, and who valued that reputation little enough to take absolutely no pains to preserve it.

It is evident to anyone watching the case from first to last that the girl earnestly desired to quit the theatre; that she hated the business; that she hoped marriage would intervene and rescue her from the life she was leading; that she was usually in high spirits but like all such was subject to depression; that in spite of all, circumstances were conspiring to force her back into the hated life of the theatre; that while a girl without a reputation in Dawson, at least, she deserved one. Fiction even does not contain an account of anything similar.

§

The *Nugget*, indeed, was Myrtle's friend. It also showed compassion in its coverage of the death of Stella Hill although the lengthy, descriptive headlines which appeared were rather flamboyant.

THE KLONDIKE NUGGET   December, 1898

Death by Strychnine Route
Stella Hill Got Tired of Life
Jealousy the Possible Cause
Has Tried it Before
The Most Rapid Case of Strychnine Poisoning on Record

The pressure of living with the Arctic region proved too much and in the presence of would-be rescuers, she took the deadly draught and ended her earthly troubles. While the contemplation of suicide as a means to an end has probably occupied her mind many times before, it remained for the concomitant circumstances of last evening to bring her resolution to a focus and her physical condition at the time made the act the most rapid of which we have any cognizance.

§

The paper said Stella was a dancer at the Monte Carlo and excellent in the art of terpsichore. Her real name was Kitty Stroup and she came from Boon's Ferry, Oregon; she had been living with Charlie Hill, a bartender at the Pioneer. After dancing all night as usual and cashing in a successful night's checks, she proceeded light-heartedly to the Pioneer in search of Charlie where she was told that he had left with another girl.

Stella walked to a waterfront drugstore where she asked the assistant for strychnine, explaining that she wanted it to kill rats and mice that were getting into her room and eating the brightly-coloured, spangled dresses she wore dancing at the Monte Carlo. The storekeeper reported she appeared quite calm and signed her name in the register with a steady hand for an eight-ounce bottle of the poison.

She went back to the Monte Carlo and said goodbye to other dancers and habitues with such a strange air of finality that the manager decided she shouldn't be left alone. He took her to her room, but when left alone inside for a few seconds she made her move.

She at once locked the door and speaking through the partition she bade neighboring roomers goodbye. At this moment Charlie arrived on the scene and being advised of the circumstances pushed in the door. As it burst open the small crowd assembled saw the girl standing in the room, holding a glass of colorless liquid. As they entered the doorway she drank hastily and threw herself on the bed with the remarks: "I have taken care of myself and now it is all done."

The doctor was sent for and forced her to drink some liquids, but in a few minutes she had a spasm and died.

Stella had arrived in Juneau as a teenager and worked for a time at Forty Mile on the Yukon River, a small mining town that was mostly abandoned when gold was struck at Dawson. She was tall with light brown hair. Away from the bright lights of the dance halls, the rhythm of the music, the free-wheeling, free-spending miners, it was a tough life for Stella. The *Nugget* said she was subject to fits of depression and had attempted suicide at least once before. It added: "She was not a heavy drinker as a rule and from custom could take a great many drinks without showing any evidence."

In the minutes when she was alone in her room, she hastily scribbled a note to her lover. It said: " Dear Charlie: I am disgusted with life since you deceived me and I guess you will be sorry when you find me." On the back was a note to her brother. Stella Hill or Kitty Stroup was 19 or 20.

A double fatality, a murder/suicide, concerned an actress at the Monte Carlo. It was said she had been drinking "considerably" in the course of the night and went to her room about seven in the morning. Her lover went into the room, shot her, shot himself and fell over the body. Maude Roselle was about 25 and Henry Davis was a 30-year-old office cashier.

THE KLONDIKE NUGGET December, 1898

Side by Side in the Grave
Hundreds of People Listen to the Services
and Look Upon the Dead Faces for the Last Time

The last earthly act in the tragedy which began unfolding when Henry Davis met Maude Roselle transpired on Sunday afternoon last when the dead bodies of the two, all that was left of the once happy pair, were laid side by side in a common grave. The woman had ceased to cherish the love that once possessed her and the man had ruthlessly destroyed her life when it had just awakened to the full sense of the possibility.

The funeral services were conducted at the Pioneer Hall which was crowded to the door while the sidewalk adjacent held those who could not find ingress.

The two bodies reposed in beautifully dressed caskets. One was draped in rich white plush and the form within was likewise clothed in white; the other in deep contrast was in black as was the silent occupant within.

§

Christmas 1898

The Episcopal Church was host to some 40 Dawson youngsters at Christmas. The party was simple and they were entertained by gramophone music and a magic lantern show. The ladies of the church laid on the event helped by the generosity of the city merchants.

THE KLONDIKE NUGGET December, 1898
The Christmas Tree
The Christmas tree which stood in the corner of the church was beautifully decorated with strings of popcorn, sacks of candies and other ornaments suitable for the occasion, and was beautifully illuminated with a number of wax candles. There was a present on the tree for every child and each one received in remembrance a sack of candies.

§

THE KLONDIKE NUGGET December, 1898
Merry Christmas
The Nugget extends to all its readers and friends in the city and on the creeks the wish for a happy and joyous Christmas. With most of us there will be a great many of the customary features lacking in the celebrations this year. Nevertheless, we can take

pleasure in celebrating the joys of former years and look forward to similar occasions in the future when again old ties and friendships will be renewed.

Yet the Christmas season even on the Klondike will be filled with pleasurable events and if our advice is taken we are of the opinion that the recurrence of our greatest holiday in this year of our Lord, 1898, will be an occasion long to be remembered. The best we can wish for our friends is a Merry Christmas, a prosperous season and a handsome clean-up in the spring.

§

Dawson's Rocket Still Burns Brightly

By the winter of 1898-99 almost anything was available in Dawson for a price. There were saloons and dance halls up and down the main streets. Entertainment changed regularly. New buildings were still going up and businesses opening. This is how the *Nugget* described the new Melbourne Hotel which opened at Second Avenue and Third Street, "in the heart of the business section."

THE KLONDIKE NUGGET   December, 1898
New Melbourne Hotel

Were it not for the exterior being built of logs one would think themselves within the extravagantly furnished apartment of one of New York's famous hostelries when in Biel's Melbourne Hotel.

A well stocked bar contains the finest lines of imported and domestic liquors and cigars and is in charge of a most accomplished mixicologist.

The second and third floors contain 16 rooms furnished in the most elaborate fashion. One suite would rival the Waldorf Astoria. It is richly papered with gilt curtain poles, elegant plush portieres, a floor covering that is a large wolverine rug and handsome bedroom suites are items of grace and elegance which invite the visitor.

Each room is furnished with full suites of furniture and the best of box mattresses and beds that money can buy. The furnishings were selected and placed by Mrs. Humphreys, a lady of charm, money and most perfect taste and the hotel portion is in her hands.

The hotel is already well filled and no more comfortable place is in the whole Northwest. Electric bells connect each room to the office and the building is lit brilliantly with acetylene gas from a private plant.

§

News from the Dawson Court House, as the new year began, contained its usual commentary on the down and out, the poor, the starving and, in one case, the ungrateful.

THE KLONDIKE NUGGET   January, 1899
Court News

Robert Russell got 18 months on the woodpile and really deserved more. When he was broke and sick he was nursed back to health in the police hospital and afterwards given employment in the officers' mess room. He responded by stealing everything in sight after but four days. The woodpile at temperatures of 50 below may work reformation.

§

By June, 1899, many goods and services were available in Dawson, but there were few permanent buildings. This "Seattle Grocery Store" was operated by I. Newens. (COURTESY SPECIAL COLLECTIONS DIVISION, UNIVERSITY OF WASHINGTON LIBRARIES, NEGATIVE UW 12851.)

Sophistication had finally come to the frontier community and some, although not all, considered it an improvement.

THE KLONDIKE NUGGET											January, 1899
Changing Times
If the gathering of the ladies and gentlemen at the Dawson Club on Wednesday night exemplifies one thing more than another, it is the rapidity of our times. Ladies in full toilette and gentlemen in high collars, patent leather shoes and black clothes where a year ago mackinaws and mukluks prevailed.

Many of our frontiersmen would admit the refinements of civilization are not really altogether favorable. Undoubtedly, with broadcloth came more intense competition for ground and for labor, and many miners mourn the fact that wages have gone down to barely the cost of living simultaneously with the introduction of the three-inch starched collar.

§

THE KLONDIKE NUGGET											January, 1899
Sally Ann
The Salvation Army is doing some very good and unostentatious work with their shelter. Some 70 meals were served last week and work is growing by reason of the acceptance of convalescent scurvy patients recommended by the relief committee.

§

FATHER WILLIAM JUDGE

Father Judge was a Baltimore-born Jesuit priest. In the eyes of all Yukoners of all denominations and those of none, he deserved the title "Saint of Dawson." An architect before he joined the order, he first came to Alaska as a missionary. The privation he suffered in the following years ruined his health but couldn't stop him. He worked tirelessly and built a hospital and church in Dawson. But the north took its toll — in his 40s he looked as if he were 60.

THE KLONDIKE NUGGET January, 1899
The Rev. Father Judge is No More
Father Judge as we all loved to call him, both Catholics and Protestants alike, died at the hospital he had cared for so long and so lovingly. The Father's faith was as real as his Christianity and almost his last words to his friends around the bed were 'This is the happiest moment of my life. I have worked for this for many years. I am going to my reward.' It was his 49th birthday.

§

Stampeders from Forty Mile to the Klondike in the winter of 1897 remembered overtaking a solitary old man (he was then 46) with a single rope sled over his shoulder and a single dog helping his load along. While others rushed to the new Dawson in pursuit of gold, Father Judge hauled medical supplies and other essentials in his sled. He made a return trip to bring more and set about building his two-storey hospital and church. His church burned down, but he uncomplainingly rebuilt it, helped with cash and labour from the many who admired him.

When the new church was completed, the *Nugget* reported on the first service.

THE KLONDIKE NUGGET   September, 1898

New Church Opens

The Rev. Father Judge would like the public to know that a week from Sunday the new Catholic Church will be open. The music for the service is now in rehearsal. How the church was built is well known to everyone but it still has to be furnished. On the occasion of the first service, the custom of the church will be departed from and a collection taken up.

§

Father William Judge built a new church beside St. Mary's Hospital, after the first church burned down. (COURTESY SPECIAL COLLECTIONS DIVISION, UNIVERSITY OF WASHINGTON LIBRARIES, NEGATIVE UW 8033.)

A quote from one *Nugget* editorial explains how the man earned his title. It had this to say about his hospital: "In the first place it is entirely non-denominational. In the second place no man, be he white, black or yellow - be he millionaire claim holder or busted prospector - was ever refused entrance to those hospitable doors."

It seemed that all of Dawson turned out for his funeral. His beloved church could hold no more. Even in the depth of winter, many, unable to get inside, stood outside during the service. Saloons, shops and commercial operations closed their doors that day. Some houses were draped in black. There were more volunteers than needed but it took diggers almost three days to hack his grave out of the frozen ground. All of Dawson did all that was possible to pay full homage to its "Saint."

They remembered him as the *Nugget* pointed out: "Delicate in health and frail in body from his early youth ... it was apparent that those he attended were healthier or stronger or suffered less than himself."

SALOONS

In Dawson the saloons often including gambling tables and dance floors and the theatres were places of refuge for many lonely and dispirited men. They were crowded, noisy, smoky; the pianos plunked until all hours, vast amounts of gold dust and nuggets changed hands, the whiskey often was rotgut and expensive and the girls always were happy to part a man from his money. A couple of whirls round the floor with one of the lovelies cost a dollar. One dancing fool blew thousands in a few days. Companionship was much sought after, and it was expensive.

Some of the establishments were rough and ready, hastily thrown together from rough lumber. Others had large mirrors, lots of brass and expensive curtains, and were a match for any of the plush premises of San Francisco. There were many saloons and they changed hands frequently. Some of the better ones were the Dominion, owned by Harry Ash; the Northern, owned by Tex Rickard; the Monte Carlo, owned by Jack Smith and the Pioneer owned by Harry Spencer. In appearance and operation they were similar and this is how Gene Allen described them to his biographer, Russell Bankson: "Inside the door and along the left-hand wall would be the long bar, with several bartenders behind it to serve the thirsty patrons. On the bar would be the delicately balanced gold scales, usually a set for each bartender. Some of these bars were grand affairs, but the back bar would be a gorgeous affair with plate-glass mirrors. The floor of the place would be pine lumber sawed in the portable mills about

Dawson City and planed down smooth; the place would be lighted with heavy oil-burning lamps suspended from the ceiling.

"The gambling room would be on the right-hand side, usually an indistinguishable part of the great saloon. And there was always found the faro bank, which was the popular game of the miners; the roulette wheels with their dealers and their lookouts, there to see that the dealer took what belonged to the house, and to settle disputes between the players; the poker wins; stud and draw, the black jack games, craps, and anything else that anyone wanted to bet on. The house put a limit on bets, but sometimes this was lifted and then things busted wide open.

"I've seen as high as $21,000 lost in a play on the roulette wheel, and as much as $5,000 at stud poker at one sitting, and I've watched men shoot dice at $1,000 a pass, just like buying a ticket for a Ladies Aid raffle.

"Two of the boys who stood out as shining examples to all poker players in the Klondike were Sam Bonnifield, who owned the Bank Saloon, and Harry Woolrich, a professional gambler who was so good that lots of bum players staked him, standing losses and dividing winnings. [These were the same two who befriended Myrtle Brocee, prior to her suicide.] They would sit for forty-eight hours straight running, til one or the other gave up, maybe a loser by thousands of dollars. When the lid popped off a game the word went around and the crowd began to close in on the players. As the stakes on the table piled up, it would get stiller, and watchers stood with glistening eyes and tense muscles while fortune wavered on the spin of a wheel, roll of the dice or turn of a card.

"Faro bank was the squarest of the mechanical games and the common herd played it the most, betting anything from fifty cents to small fortunes on the showing of a card as it was drawn from the box.

"And right here I want to say, by the way, I got it from the operators of gambling games, themselves, no matter how honest and fair a gambling game is operated, the percentage is always in favor of the house, because the players will stay to lose by digging down for another try, but will quit with a quick winning.

"By that I mean a man will place a bet on a spin of the wheel or turn of the card and if he wins he will feel satisfied that he is ahead of the game and quit. But if he loses the first time he will try to make up the loss by playing again, and like as not keep it up until he's broke.

"Leaving the gambling hall there'd be a door that led to the dancehall or variety theatre, which would also be connected with the barroom by a door. This is where the dancehall girls congregated for the entertainment of the male guests.

"If it was a variety hall there would be a stage at the rear, where the girls would put on dancing and singing acts, after which they would mingle with the patrons, dancing with them and leading them to the bar to buy drinks. If it was a dancehall only, the patrons danced with the girls without cost, then led them to the bar and bought drinks for themselves and the girls. The girls would take ginger ale and the men straight whiskey. They were small drinks but they cost one dollar. Twenty-five cents of this went to the girl, the rest to the house.

"The dancehalls had good floors and fine orchestras. Pianos were brought in by boat, and there would also be violins, drums, banjos and horns. Some of the musicians had played in the best orchestras in the States, but had gotten the gold fever and ended up in the dancehalls.

"Most of the dance floors had plenty of room and were lined around the walls with a mezzanine balcony of private boxes. Men who wanted privacy could use these boxes and by drawing the curtains be shut off from the rest of the crowd, or by opening them they could watch the show on the stage or the dancers below. Some of the girls worked the boxes by visiting the guests who paid twice the regular prices for their drinks and smokes.

"For the most part the dancehall girls were honest, protecting the gold sacks of the drunken miners and they were not vulgarly lewd. Their aim and objective was to sell drinks and as a rule they 'lived privately' - that is, they were not of the bawdy house type.

"Bawdy house girls were in another and much lower class by themselves and the dancehall girls, who considered themselves artists, had nothing to do with them.

"The good old-fashioned dances were the most popular. The miners and the stampeders loved the schottische, the polka, the square dance and such. The Blue Danube Waltz was all the rage and you could hear it 24 hours a day. The Merry Widow Waltz and Turkey in the Straw were other favorites. The callers for the dances were usually old timers who knew their stuff, had good voices and a flare for humor.

"Some of the larger houses would have 20 or 30 girls to entertain their patrons. The crowds in the dancehalls ran from the 'dudes' in their tailored clothes to the miners and muckers just in from the creeks with their parkas and moccasins on. News of a new strike or big cleanup always spread like wildfire and when someone with a heavy sack showed up in a dancehall, the girls mobbed him, making him feel like he was an Arabian Sheik.

"Lots of times when a miner struck it rich he'd come in and buy out a dancehall, or a whole saloon, for an hour or a night and invite his friends to celebrate with him.

"The saloons and gambling rooms kept going 24 hours a day, but the dancehalls didn't really wake up until evening. Where there were variety shows, the performers did their stuff in the evening, then the dancing started and kept on into the next morning as long as there was anyone to dance.

"Like any place that is wide open and wild, there were plenty of parasites — the shark gamblers, the cheap grafters and the bunco artists, both men and women. In the Klondike these took a good slice of the gold dust that was washed from the creeks.

"Considering though the usually loose morals of such stampede camps, and the traps laid for the ones who made their cleanups, it is surprising so many actually did come out of the Klondike with stakes large and small."[4]

Joaquin Miller

One of the more eccentric residents of Dawson was a man named Joaquin (also Joseph) Miller, sometimes called "The Poet of the Sierra Nevada."
Miller appeared in a vaudeville performance at Palmer's Theatre in New York when he was well along in years. Each evening the old man walked on stage at nine o'clock, dressed from head to foot in furs to give a short talk and read poetry on Klondike affairs.
R. C. Kirk, a Dawson resident, attended one of the New York shows and reported that it was a popular one. The theatre might be half empty up to nine o'clock, but then there would be a rush and the place would fill to the doors to hear Miller's poetry readings. Audiences often listened in silence to the very end of his performance, the quiet broken only by an occasional burst of applause. He was also well known to readers of the *Nugget*.

THE KLONDIKE NUGGET   January, 1899
Comrades of the Klondike
To Sam C. Dunham
Have you too banged at the Chilcoot -
That storm-locked gate to the golden door;
Those thunder-built steeps have words built to suit
And whether you prayed or whether you swore

T'were one, where it seemed that an oath were a prayer-
Seem'd that God couldn't care -Seem'd that God wasn't there!
Have you, too, climbed to the Klondike?
Hast talked as a friend to the five-horned czars?
With muckluck, piton and tailspike,
Hast bared grey head to the golden bars-
The heaven-built bars, where morning is born?
Hast drank with Maiden Morn
From Klondike's golden horn?
Hast read low-voiced by the northern lights,
Such sermons as never men say?
Hast sat and sat with the midnights
That sit and that sit all day?
Hast heard the silence - the room -
The glory of God - the gloom -
Then come to my sun-land my soldier!
Aye, come to my heart and to stay -
Young hand! For a better - a bolder -
Bared never his heart to the fray
And, whether you prayed or you cursed -
You dare the best and worst
That ever brave men doeth!

Joseph Miller

§

THE KLONDIKE NUGGET								January, 1899

Reply

I, too, have banged at the Chilcoot -
I have scaled her storm-torn heights -
And slid down her trail with dizzy shoot,
That produced a northern "lights";
Of course, God didn't care,
For only the Devil was there.
I, too, have climbed the Klondike
Thro' bog and muck and roots,
Till my legs were stiff as the tailspike
And the water filled both of my boots;
Have drunk from the golden horn,
With maidens night and morn -
I acknowledged the corn;

"Dear Little Nugget"

Have heard the loud-voiced by the north lights
Such oaths as only men say;
Have laid awake thro' the midnight,
And fought mosquitoes all day;
Curse Klondike - not the icebergs - boom.
And paid an ounce for a room.
Which filled my soul with gloom.
My friend, I'll come to the sun-land
As soon as this long winter's o'er,
And I'll drink to thy health in the one land
Whither thy thoughts ever soar;
And tho' this drought be the worst
That ever humanity cursed,
At last we'll banish our thirst.

Sam C. Dunham

§

Staff of the Nugget *in the winter of 1898-99. (Photo by E.A. Hebb, from* The Klondike Nugget, by Russell Bankson.*)*

The Final Year of the Century Begins

As the final year of the old century began, the community of Dawson basked in the glow of gold and stories of great riches. There seemed to be no signs of change and many believed that, for them, prosperity was just around the corner. The *Nugget* continued to chronicle events and pastimes in this isolated community with its unusual heroes.

THE KLONDIKE NUGGET   February, 1899
Court News
G. Wells carefully stretched his stomach over a too great measure of liquid happiness and collapsed. Not having $20 left he will cut wood for 20 days at the rate of $2 per day. They don't pay very good wages on the woodpile.

§

THE KLONDIKE NUGGET   February, 1899
The Value of a Dog
W. Reeder paid $25 and costs and also the value of the dead dog for having filled him with lead somewhere on Dominion last week. The value allowed for the defunct canine was $75. The dog was looting Mr. Reader's cache and the owner of the disappearing bacon awaited

the thief with a gun. Justice Starnes took the occasion to advise the defendant that as dogs were a necessary evil in this country, he should have not taken the law into his own hands.

§

THE KLONDIKE NUGGET   February, 1899

Advertisement
50 Cents Buys the Best
Meal in Dawson
at the
Rainier House
A clean and commodious bunk house
Waterfront

§

THE KLONDIKE NUGGET   February, 1899

Unhappy Mrs. Schwartz

A sensational episode found the scene of the action at the store of the Northwest Trading Company when Mrs. Joseph Schwartz with fire flashing from her coal black eyes and an improvised rope whip in her hands suddenly appeared on the scene and made an effort to apply her weapon to the retreating figure of Joseph Kleinberg. The gentleman's agility and masterful strategy defeated the design of the angry woman and she perforce gave him a vigorous tongue lashing in lieu of the other means with which she sought to allay her wrath. The incident is due to the fact that Mr. Kleinberg while conversing with Pat Biel passed a remark that was derogatory to her dignity.

§

THE KLONDIKE NUGGET   February, 1899

Advertisement
Go where good things await you,
Where good cooking will elate you,
Where cleanliness is manifest,
And the menu is the very best.
To find the place where such is true,
Go to the Cafe Royale on Second Avenue.

§

THE KLONDIKE NUGGET   March, 1899

Dog Race

Considerable interest was manifested Sunday afternoon in a race between two teams of dogs owned by Bob Aisley and W. L'heureux. The course was the trail from the mouth of Hunker to Dawson, a distance of 10 miles and the stakes were $100 a side with many times that amount put up by the friends and partisans of the two principals. No less than 2,000 people lined the river at the goal to see the final. (L'heureux won in a time of 45 minutes and 10 seconds.)

§

THE KLONDIKE NUGGET   March, 1899

Real Estate

West Dawson has been plotted and placed on the market giving an opportunity for Dawsonites to acquire a home in a locality where spontaneous sickness is almost unknown, air is found fresh, there is an abundance of pure, sweet water and where the drainage keeps the ground dry throughout the summer. The site is the most picturesque imaginable and it affords people to escape from the pestilential atmosphere that will make a plague spot of Dawson in the coming year. A ferry boat will be operating and a trip will be made every half hour. The present lots are being held at exceedingly reasonable rates and even for speculators buyers are promised a good buy. Sickness in Dawson is destined to bring about a stampede to this garden spot.

§

THE KLONDIKE NUGGET   March, 1899

Gold Value

M. Marks, a well-known Dawsonite who lately went outside, has furnished Seattle papers with an estimate of the Klondike's output for this season as follows: Eldorado, $2,500,000; Bonanza, $2,500,000; French Hill, $1,600,000; Gold Hill, $1,500,000; Big Skookum, $1,000,000; Little Skookum, $1,000,000; Dominion, $4,000,000; Hunker and Quartz, $5,000,000.

§

While some people still insisted on doing their business in nuggets and gold dust, many were much relieved when the Bank of Commerce arrived and brought a semblance of normal business practice to the Yukon. It was

Miners waiting for the bank to open so that their gold dust could be weighed and assessed. (COURTESY SPECIAL COLLECTIONS DIVISION, UNIVERSITY OF WASHINGTON LIBRARIES, NEGATIVE UW 12831.)

badly needed because "salting" gold dust with worthless sand dropped its value to much less than the going rate of about $16 an ounce.

The Bank of Commerce realized early that there was money to be made in Dawson, and a six-man crew left Toronto for the far northwest in April of 1898. They went over the White Pass but had a problem that few had on the trail. When they passed through Skagway en route, they had to disguise the case in which they were carrying the paper money. It was hidden for fear that Soapy Smith and his Skagway gang would make a move on it. Soapy never knew, however, and the money arrived in Dawson safely. All the team arrived by June 14 and the Commerce was in business the next day. They quickly found how much the dust had been tampered with by "salting" and subsequently had to write off a five-figure sum (a lot of money in those days) for over-valued dust held in their safe. The miners, or most of them, caught on to the advantage of using paper money and soon there was a premium of about ten per cent; a paper dollar cost one dollar and ten cents in gold dust.

The bank was doing a roaring business with long line-ups outside waiting for the doors to open each day. Another small problem not usually encountered by bankers was trying to get sleep — they lived over the "store" — despite the sounds of the noisy roistering and late-late-night partying on the streets by a lively section of the population.

The Commerce continues in Dawson to this day, but a highlight of its history was the transfer to its Whitehorse branch in 1904 of a young man named Robert W. Service. The heyday of the Yukon was actually over by the time the man who became known as its Bard arrived there. While in Whitehorse, Service wrote poems and entertained at social functions by giving readings. He moved to the Dawson branch in 1908 but by this time he was starting to get world-wide acclaim for his writing, and soon after, he gave up banking.

Other items from the *Nugget* in March, 1899, included the following:

THE KLONDIKE NUGGET   March, 1899
Hockey
The match between the Dawson Hockey Club and the Canadian Permanent Force Hockey Club which took place Saturday at the skating rink resulted in a victory for the Permanent Force by five goals to one. The game was very fast and at the end of the first half there was little to choose between the two teams, the score standing at one all. The Dawson Club weakened in the second half and the Permanent Force took their chances and did some good combined play.

§

THE KLONDIKE NUGGET   March, 1899
Ancient Horns
A curiosity dug from the earth at a depth of 21 feet at 10A Sulphur was brought to town Wednesday afternoon and is now at the warehouse of the N.A.T. & T. Co. It consists of a pair of large horns, attached to a fraction of skull, and is undoubtedly the mortal remains of a species of quadruped belonging to prehistoric days; in fact, Mr. D. G. Frazier, on whose claim it was unearthed, says it belongs to what was undoubtedly the original ox. The animal to which the horns belonged, judging from the size, must have weighed from 2,500 to 3,000 pounds.

§

THE KLONDIKE NUGGET   March, 1899
Not So Cold as it Seems
The first four days of the past week have demonstrated again what we have often maintained that the absence of numerous

reliable thermometers makes it comparatively easy for stories of extreme cold to originate in this land of continuous cold temperatures. A sharp breeze of from eight to 10 miles an hour affected us for four days and nights and many men who had hitherto escaped the ravages of Jack Frost succumbed to his ruthless might and for three days have been engaged in doctoring nipped faces and hands for the first time this winter. Thermometers are nowadays quite common and it took constant reference to them to rid one of the impression that the temperature was at least 60 below, while as a matter of fact it was hovering at 30 below. But for the reassuring presence of the thermometer, on many a diary would be written: Feb. 27, Monday, 60 below.

§

BIG ALEX

Big Alex McDonald was indeed a giant of a man who hailed from Nova Scotia. He was in the Klondike when the gold was found in '96 and moved rapidly to stake his claim and acquire those of others who decided to sell out. He became known as the "King of the Klondike" and achieved world-wide fame, at least for a little while. At one point he was said to be worth about $20,000,000 and offered a jar of gold nuggets to visitors as though they were chocolates.

Like many others he died fairly young and a millionaire no more, his money gone in various schemes and failed enterprises, but in early '99 he was "King." On his first trip to London he married 20-year-old Margaret Chisholm.

THE KLONDIKE NUGGET   February, 1899

King of the Klondike Marries

When he left Dawson he had two letters, one from Miss Chisholm of this city and the other for the father of Miss Chisholm in London. The name of Chisholm became identified in the Klondiker's mind with fascinating femininity and it did not take him long after meeting with the London girl to decide that he need look no further for a charming wife. When Miss Chisholm of this city, who is a stenographer in the controller's office, was informed of the wealthy marriage of her English namesake, she smiled and said, "Well, it's all in the family." One would have to describe Miss Chisholm as a good sport.

§

The *Nugget* didn't say how McDonald got the letter of introduction to the London girl, or if he had known the Miss Chisholm of Dawson. It reported that the London wedding attracted a lot of young people to the church who didn't want so much to see the bride or the ceremony but to see one of the famous miners who had struck it so very, very rich in the Klondike.

Big Alex couldn't stay away long from the goldfield and his many interests. In April the *Nugget* carried this story:

THE KLONDIKE NUGGET   April, 1899
    Big Alex McDonald Came Back With
    His Bride But Left Her in Massachusetts.

His restless and prudent spirit could not tolerate so much idleness so he left Mrs. McDonald in Massachusetts (with a relative) and came on alone. McDonald is credited with having broken the record for the journey having made the trip in just 11 days. He appeared none the worst for his rapid pace and our Nugget man thinks it did him good and he is in the pink of condition. He used horses for a large share of the way and dogs for the balance.

    The experiences of his journey included a shipwreck, the Topeka, on which he sailed from Seattle with 100 other passengers, having run afoul of some rocks near Wrangell. She was rapidly filling with water when a government boat came up and took the passengers off. He didn't learn the fate of the wrecked steamer but thinks she must have gone to the bottom.

§

McDonald's wife followed later when the ice broke and the river was navigable. When he died several years later, Big Alex's vast fortune was gone but he was still prospecting. He was found dead outside his cabin on Clearwater Creek, having suffered a heart attack. An insurance policy he had been talked into buying provided his widow with a reasonable income.

Big Alex was not the only famous millionaire, just the best known. Many others were also considered "rich."

THE KLONDIKE NUGGET   April, 1899
The Rich

This week saw the arrival from the outside of several well-known sourdoughs, including Charles Anderson, John Lee, J.R. Nixon and Mr. Williams. The first named became one of the best known of early Klondikers by reason of having as the story goes, been made a victim of two sharpers at Forty-Mile, who sold him No 29 Eldorado for $800. The next day, Charlie tried to recover his money, but he failed and now he is glad of it for 29 is one of the richest claims on Eldorado and he is rated among the millionaires. He is also a half-owner with Mr. Lee in No. 32. While on the outside, Mr. Anderson purchased a country seat 15 miles north of San Francisco and three miles from San Rafael, for which he paid $19,000. Charlie is still a heart-free bachelor, but with such attractive encumbrances as attached to him now he has become too good a catch to escape the pitfalls which cupid will dig in his path.

§

Les Girls — A Fact of Life

Appreciating that prostitution was a fact of life and an important one in an isolated town where men outnumbered women by up to 25 to one, the *Nugget*, nevertheless, felt that there was a time and place, particularly the latter, for everything.

THE KLONDIKE NUGGET   April, 1899
Progress Wins the Day
The thread which has so long held the official axe over the famous tenderloin district has snapped asunder, the inexorable demands of progress have won the day. No longer may the women in scarlet occupy the choicest of city lots and flaunt crimson colors on Dawson's crowded streets, no longer may the seductive window tap beguile the innocent prospector or hurrying man of business. The reign of the scarlet letter is on the wane, one of the institutions most cherished and nourished in halcyon days of yore is about to be degraded.

§

Readers were told that Second Avenue had to be severed from its old ways of life in the interests of morality and business, but obviously not necessarily in that order.

THE KLONDIKE NUGGET   April, 1899
Waterfront to be Cleared

It had to come. The clearing of the waterfront, the growing population, the increasing business interests, the demand for better public morals. The 300 or so representatives of the demi-monde have been notified that they will no longer be tolerated on the prominent business streets and in the alleys. After May 1st they must occupy quarters less conspicuous and convenient.

§

The *Nugget* said it was understood that the "sisterhood would be confined to the area between Fourth and the east end." However, business interests and public morals seem to have come to a happy resolution. The *Nugget* said approval had been given to a well-known business firm to build a large tenement building "for the accommodation of such as prefer the economy which goes with that class of structure."

THE CONSUL AND THE KICKS

Even for the Phoenix dance hall and saloon it was unusual for the U.S. consul to Dawson to be there with a small Stars and Stripes flag fastened to the seat of his pants, inviting patrons to give him a kick in the rear. The subsequent blow-up between Consul J. C. McCook and the *Nugget* resulted in great hilarity for *Nugget* readers throughout the Klondike in the spring of '99. It was the sort of tale in which Gene Allen delighted, funny and satisfying because he won a libel suit brought against him by the unfortunate consul.

It began when McCook spoke at a dinner for the retiring Klondike Gold Commissioner, Thomas Fawcett, the *Nugget*'s arch enemy and the man it had fought long and hard to have replaced. He didn't say all that much, but the paper didn't like it and editorialized to that effect. Then followed a long series of letters of complaint from McCook and testy rejoinders by the *Nugget*. It wound up with the consul suing for damages. Poor McCook was undone by an unfortunate small-hours visit to the Phoenix where he went down in flames and did not rise from the ashes. The story became the talk and the joke of the Klondike. With the consul at its mercy, the *Nugget* didn't miss a trick and pulled out all the stops. McCook's downfall was described in typical *Nugget* style:

THE KLONDIKE NUGGET   April, 1899
Consul Makes Spectacle of Himself
Consul J. C. McCook, the American representative to the Yukon Territory constituting the buffoon of a dance hall crowd while in a state of intoxication, was a lamentable spectacle witnessed at the Phoenix on Thursday morning last.

§

The story of the disgraceful affair flew through town like wildfire and was on everybody's lips by nightfall. The *Nugget* somewhat unctuously said it knew of the affair but elected not to write about it until a police enquiry was completed. It was then that a detailed story appeared:

THE KLONDIKE NUGGET   April, 1899
McCook the Patriot
Mr. McCook arrived at the Phoenix at a late hour of the morning under the influence of a heavy "jar". He was inclined to be merry and out for a good time. McCook became a super patriot and took offence when a young Canadian said he wasn't an American. He rushed the young dissenter but was separated by bar staff and owner Pete McDonald.

The consul then tried to show that his heart was in the right place by ordering a fresh round every time anybody declared himself or herself to be an American, for by that time the girls had been attracted from the dance hall and gathered around the celebrator. But he could not overlook or forgive the temerity of his late adversary who had presumed to declare his allegiance to the Queen, and the additional drinks had put the Consul in a state of utter recklessness.

McCook went after the Canadian again. Their manoeuvres finally landed them in the dance hall where they fell to the floor, with Peter, the night porter, "who was not sober himself by that time," on top of them. A couple of interested spectators took hold of these squirming men by the heels and dragged them into the bar room where they were disentangled, and again the bloody chasm was bridged by the flowing bowl.

The consul then turned his attention to show that he "knows a pretty girl when he sees her...." The gallant McCook unfastened his gold watch from its chain and gave it to Nellie James. This special mark of his favor made the other girls jealous and disgruntled and in order to placate the beauties he proceeded to distribute among them a choice collection of gold nuggets which he had about his person. His unexpected generosity seemed to grow with the giving, indeed, for he suddenly threw up both hands and invited the girls to help themselves to anything they could find: "Take the whole works!" he exclaimed encouragingly. The girls could not withstand such eloquent and manly persuasion and they soon had the pockets of his coat, vest and pants turned inside out.

It was during the general hilarity that someone attached the Stars and Stripes to the seat of his pants. It may have been this which inspired the consul with a most original idea for contributing further to the amusement of the crowd. Taking hold of the bar railing he bent forward and then called, "Kick me, Pete." This referred to the aforesaid night porter, who not wishing to disappoint the expectant throng, several times planted the toe of his boot against the consul's posterior. The effect was so extremely delightful to the consul that he urged Pete to still greater exertions and being willing to oblige to the extent of his power, the porter would start on the run from the other side of the room and send the consul over the bar with the force of the impact between shoe leather and tweed worsted.

This went on for some time until the consul begged permission to retire. It was a difficult accomplishment alone, and two men — each holding an arm — accompanied him to the back door, past the row of bawdy houses, and down the alley to Second Street, where he was left to make his way as best he could to his room. Genuine hardship here befell him, for he met with a chilly rebuke from a girl whose "cigar store" he attempted to enter, lost his equilibrium and fell to earth. He made several heroic but vain attempts to arise, but being unable to, he finally resigned himself to his fate and crawled on his hands and knees across the muddy alley, up on the sidewalk, to the door leading to his office building .... Only the consul and his Maker, possibly, knew how the final journey up the two flights of steep stairs to his room was accomplished.

§

It was a bad night for diplomacy and McCook. Nellie James turned over the watch and it was returned to the consul later that day, but his watch chain was missing and police were called. It wasn't found.

A *Nugget* editorial later flayed the poor man further, waxed indignant again and commented: "By the shade of the immortal George Washington, we conjure you to drop the position in which you make every proud American in the land to hang his head in very shame ... make a small sacrifice of your salary for the honor of your country and

Americans temporarily dwelling in a strange land will only too willingly forget the mortification of their feelings, which you have subjected them to."

The *Nugget* certainly was having fun with poor McCook and readers loved it. McCook didn't. He brought a criminal libel charge against Allen. It was standing room only in the court for the trial on May 30.

Those who came for the laughs weren't disappointed. It also was fairly clear on whose side rested the jury. In an hour they came back and exonerated Allen and the paper. Nothing else was heard of the other actions raised by the consul. The *Nugget* took another editorial kick at the unfortunate man, and shortly afterwards he said a quiet farewell to Dawson, his night at the Phoenix being added to the list of great yarns of the days when Dawson was, indeed, wild and woolly.

IN THE SPRING OF THE YEAR

As the spring of the year 1899 arrived, events in Dawson moved at a faster pace, like the winter's ice as it cleared the Yukon River. Everyone knew breakup was coming and then suddenly it happened and everything changed. People and goods were on the move along the waterways. Supplies running short after a hard winter were being replenished. Miners heard news of new gold discoveries in Alaska. There was a restless feeling in the town and out on the creeks.

THE KLONDIKE NUGGET   May, 1899
River Ice Moves
Dawson's big gala day came on Wednesday, the 17th of May, when, after weary waiting and heart-breaking anxiety, the great mass of ice which had held her bound from intercourse with all the world, broke moorings and started carrying the load of noisome filth for the open sea below.

It was a day that no one will forget, commencing the release from the thraldom that had almost reached the limit of endurance. It came at 4:15 in the afternoon so quietly as not to attract attention. Then as the motion was growing and the dark spots of dirt decking its surface were seen to move, a steamboat's whistle rent the air and a great shout went up from a hundred throats — She's going. The ice is moving.

Businesses and stores emptied as people thronged to see the action. As far as the eye could see the river was filled with rapidly-moving ice that as it increased its speed began to grind and tumble and roar and plunge like mad living things. Huge pieces of ice, weighing tons and as big as houses, were pushed high in the air. Thousands watched.

§

Reports continued to filter in of a new gold strike in Alaska and men who wanted to be among the first to a new gold find made plans to move on. Amid signs of spring and some changes on the horizon, life went on as usual in many other ways; gold was displayed, the girls in the red-light district were given an extension of time before they had to move, and the Salvation Army said the numbers of "the down and out" were on the increase and that government restrictions were making the situation worse.

THE KLONDIKE NUGGET   May, 1899
The Golden Show
Mr. Nels Peterson, the president of the Yukon Flyer Line, had an exhibition at the company office, Chisholm's Saloon, a collection of nuggets which rival that of any other collections in the country.

Winter and summer, miners roamed the streets of Dawson to catch up on the latest news, look for friends or pick up supplies to take back to the diggings.
(COURTESY SPECIAL COLLECTIONS DIVISION, UNIVERSITY OF WASHINGTON LIBRARIES, PHOTO BY E.A. HEBB, NEGATIVE 2267.)

Among the number was one of the value of $314, two others of about $186 and one of $128 and several of the value of $75 to $100 and all were taken from the famous Skookum claim discovered by Mr. Peterson and Mr. Kroeger. From this claim within six days, after they had made the discovery they rocked out $14,000.

§

THE KLONDIKE NUGGET   May, 1899
Delay
A couple of weeks ago the loose women of the town were notified that with the first of May they would be obliged to vacate the business section of the city. But owing to the subsequent fire and the fact that provisions have not been made for their reception elsewhere, they have been granted an extension of time until June.

§

THE KLONDIKE NUGGET   May, 1899
Destitution is Increasing
Adjutant McGill of the Salvation Army is of the opinion that destitution is increasing in the Klondike and hopes to see something turn up to alleviate the situation of which work would be the best. At present there are 10 men looking for every job and the outlook is for serious suffering unless something turns up. A little while back the Army had fed out all their provisions to the needy but the situation has been eased and the shelter is still keeping up its work. The situation has been increased by the late action of the government in withholding aid from the needy except in cases of sickness.

§

ALASKAN GOLD STAMPEDE

Word filtered down to Dawson that there had been a fabulous new strike some 1,500 miles away in Alaska. Once the news hit the town it spread rapidly through the streets, the saloons, the stores, and out to the creeks and the toiling miners. Simple rumours of fabulous wealth once again created the gold fever that had produced the Klondike rush. The big difference was that the latter had been backed up by the arrival in Seattle and San Francisco of tons of gold.

In mid-June the *Nugget* carried its first major story about the Alaska strike, unsure if the area was called Cape Nome or Gnome. Dawson business interests knew that it was bad news for them, and this was quickly confirmed by men striking out in small groups while others packed departing steamers.

The *Nugget* ran subsequent stories seemingly aimed at trying to take some of the shine off the reported new finds, but this event marked the beginning of Dawson's decline. In a special edition of the *Nugget* the news of the gold strike created no little excitement about town and quickly became the dominant theme of discussion. The majority of men were skeptical and many openly pronounced the story a scheme of the transportation companies to work up business for the boats.

THE KLONDIKE NUGGET   June, 1899
Gold in Alaska

Whether or not this theory is true, the Nugget does not know. Like a faithful dispenser of the news should, it gave the report as quickly as it seemed importance deserved and then only for what it was worth, naming the source from which the news emanated, the manner in which it was received in Dawson only a few hours before, and urging upon our readers to wait for a confirmation of the news before going on a stampede.

But the report was evidently received with more favorable consideration by many, for when the steamer Sovereign of the Columbia Navigation Company pulled out for St. Michael's at 8 o'clock last Saturday evening her forward space held a crowd of men and women bound for the new field.

It was a rarely edifying sight to see a steamboat load of people leaving the Klondike on a 2,000 mile stampede with little, if anything, more tangible in the way of information than the story of a sensational newspaper in Seattle and it cannot fail, when known to the outside world, to create the liveliest speculation, so little are the real conditions of this country known outside.

§

THE KLONDIKE NUGGET   July, 1899
Advertisement
Ho, for Cape Nome!
Steamer Sybil

The swiftest boat on the Yukon leaves the Yukon dock Wednesday, July 19, at 10 p.m. for St. Michael and Cape Nome

The Sybil should reach St. Michael in five days from Dawson.

This offers the very earliest opportunity for reaching the Cape Nome gold fields

§

Later in July two men known along the Yukon from Dawson to its mouth came back from a trip to Nome. They were Ed McConnell and Dan McLennan. The *Nugget* interviewed both:

THE KLONDIKE NUGGET   July, 1899
Back from Nome

McLennan — There is gold there but not in great quantity and it is a hard country to work in. The only wood is on the beach and the season is very short — everything was still frozen up when we left there on the first of July and it is hard travelling.

The niggerhead swamps of the Klondike are macadamized roads in comparison. Then the good country is taken up and practically held by five men who took lots of Laplanders and Eskquimaux in there during the winter months for the purposes of staking.

McConnell — In my opinion it is a steamboat boom and the biggest farce I ever saw. There is color everywhere in the ground but no paying gold. The best I saw was 2-cent dirt.

§

Charlie Meadows

In a town full of colourful characters, none stood out more than Charlie Meadows, a man who looked more like Buffalo Bill than Bill himself. It was an image he carefully cultivated, but Charlie did have a western background. He had lived on the prairies and was described by the *Nugget* and others as an old Indian fighter. With his flowing hair and Buffalo Bill style, he had performed with a cowboy troupe all over the world and was well versed in the art of show business. For a time he tried his hand at prospecting, but Charlie soon ascertained that he could make his bundle by catering to the entertainment needs of Dawson.

There was much enthusiasm when Charlie decided to build Dawson's first legitimate theatre. The *Nugget* got quite carried away, stating that it would hold 2,200 people. That was a slight exaggeration to say the least. They would have had to pile them up like cordwood for that, but the theatre was impressive and it soon became very popular.

THE KLONDIKE NUGGET   June, 1899

Charlie's Theatre

At last Dawson is to have a theatre. Charlie Meadows' Grand Opera Theatre is to be finished July 4. The Elks have rented the entire building for that day and night. In the afternoon they will give a good entertainment in which all the best talent in Dawson will take part and in the evening an inaugural ball will be given, the proceeds of which is to go to the sick fund.

The Grand is located on Third Street next door to Nigger Jim's Pavilion and just opposite the new post office site. The new playhouse will be a magnificent structure and one that Dawson may well be proud of.

The new pleasure palace will be a three-storey building, 40 feet wide and 180 feet long with two rows of boxes and will have capacity of 2,200 over four times the capacity of any building in town. The theatre will be used to accommodate legitimate companies for performances, socials and balls until the arrival of Charlie's special company which is now being organized in San Francisco.

The front will be a saloon, the middle floor for apartments and the top floor will be a large hall for the different fraternal orders. The fittings and furniture will be selected from the very best and latest imports from the outside. Eight hundred opera chairs have been ordered.

§

Charlie's big night finally arrived and there was the grand opening of the Grand Theatre, but as one report noted, not everyone was impressed with the performance, nor the script and songs rendered by one of the stars.

THE KLONDIKE NUGGET   July, 1899

The Grand Opens

Representatives of the nobility were there along with a good sprinkling of the 400 and a goodly proportion of sourdoughs.

There were one or two things in the performance that grated somewhat harshly upon the sensitivities of some few of the audience. For instance, in the course of the performance the beauteous fairy queen drawn on a luxurious barge by a pair of swans came on the scene. Although alighting gracefully and with all the dignity of royalty, she advanced to the front of the stage while her humble pages, drawn up on either side, did homage to their sovereign as she passed. But then instead of addressing her subjects upon grave and lofty matters of state, she turned towards the audience and regaled them with a rendition of that masterpiece of harmony and sentiment entitled — All Coons Look Alike to Me.

§

THE TELEGRAPH LINE ARRIVES

Isolation was a fact of life in early Dawson, accentuated for early arrivals by concern for their families and what was happening in the outside world. A telephone system was set up in Dawson early in its history, but it was limited to the town, with some lines extending out to the creeks. The *Nugget* got its outside news from talking to new arrivals — hence some of the reports were more than slightly inaccurate — and by out-hustling its competitors for copies of old newspapers that some people brought in with them. That's why a story of a world championship boxing match taken from a two-month-old outside paper made headline news and was avidly read by *Nugget* subscribers.

The people of Dawson pressed the government for a communication link and after the usual bureaucratic dithering and delay watched the progress as the line was driven through difficult country and over the mountains from Skagway. Readers were told of the progress and completion in the *Nugget*.

THE KLONDIKE NUGGET   June, 1899
Telegraph Line
The new Skagway-Dawson Telegraph-telephone line is completed to a point below the Whitehorse rapids. The crew is progressing at the rate of seven miles a day and is convinced that the line will be in operation by September. There is a report that the government is

watching closely the experiments being made with the new system of wireless telegraphy and its practical utility.

§

THE KLONDIKE NUGGET   September, 1899
Telegraph is in Dawson
Built in 133 Days

At last the government telegraph line into Dawson is an accomplished fact. At 5:13 p.m. Thursday the wire reached the building prepared for its arrival at the barracks and was attached to an instrument already in place and then commenced a ticking of congratulatory messages in both directions. The importance of the line to Dawson and its inhabitants creates a halo of interest in every operation of its construction.

The first pole was stuck into the ground as late as April 20 this year and its completion to Dawson on September 28 marks five months and eight days since its commencement.

§

The line ran for 600 miles. The government appropriated $147,000 for the work, which included the cost of 92 men living and working from six scows in the river. One river crossing was 350 feet without support.

In addition to the building of the telegraph, the *Nugget* reported on other important events during the summer of '99.

THE KLONDIKE NUGGET   July, 1899
Record Trip

The steamer Victoria arrived from Whitehorse Tuesday afternoon with a brand new broom sticking from the top of the pilot house. Inquiry developed the fact that the boat had beaten all previous records for the run to Whitehorse on her way up, the time being four days and two hours.

§

THE KLONDIKE NUGGET   July, 1899
The Klondike's First Elopement

The hero in this melodrama is John Orten, lately a prospector in the gold-laden gulches of the Klondike, but formerly a cowboy from the State of Montana.

Whether it is necessary to be wicked in order to be a cowboy is a mooted question, but in this instance the fact is made to apply to the prejudice of the young man.

The heroine of the romance is Miss Mabel Nummelin, a young lady who has seen but 16 summers pass over her tender head. She is of Norwegian extraction, but a native-born American. Her parents have been keeping a road house in one of the creeks.

§

The young lovers were seen fleeing down the river in an open boat, and her irate father informed police. The affair was short lived. They were found at Forty Mile where he had found work and were quickly returned to Dawson.

THREE MEN EXECUTED

The summer of 1899 saw the first hanging in Dawson and it was an event covered in detail by the *Nugget*. Three men were convicted of two different murders and all were sentenced to hang. The manner in which *Nugget* reporters covered the event was a reflection of the times.

Edward Henderson was about 30 and a native of England. Convicted of the revolver killing of a companion after a quarrel on the trail, he was in poor physical shape for the year he was in custody before his execution.

The Nantuk brothers were in their 20s and convicted of the rifle slaying of a prospector in an apparent attempt to rob him and his companion, who was only wounded. Originally, four men were arrested. One died in custody and the fourth was given a jail sentence because of his youth. The *Nugget*'s story was a lengthy one.

THE KLONDIKE NUGGET   August, 1899

Justice Finally Done
Murderers at Last Pay the Penalty of Their Crime
Two Nantuk Boys and Henderson Executed

The first official hanging which has transpired in the Yukon Territory — indeed it may be more generally said in the entire Yukon Country — will bear the date of August 4.

The victims of the same were Edward Henderson and Jim and Dawson Nantuk and all of them went to their deaths for the crime of murder.

The execution was conducted in the most private way, only a few representatives of the press, police officials, the coroner's jury, medical attendants and the necessary guards were present.

The scaffold had been constructed in the northwest corner of the barracks .... The drop consisted of a double trap door 12 feet long by three feet wide and operated by the simple movement of a lever. Above and reaching from end to end of the roof was a huge piece of timber from which the three ropes were suspended over the centre of the trap.

Henderson passed a quiet, peaceful night and his last on earth. He was deeply engrossed with the thoughts of his approaching dissolution and seemed hardly to feel the necessity of sleep. The two Indians were alone and passed the night in absolute quiet. Jim Nantuk slept for several hours.

Shortly after 7 a.m. the men were led from their cells and into the square. A wall prevented the crowd outside from viewing the scene.

As Henderson emerged into the light of day his face brightened and he looked squarely in the face of those gathered around him in a fearless yet mild and almost happy way. He walked erect with his head held high. The Indians too held up bravely and required but little support. But the spiritual control which characterized Henderson was absent from their ashen-hued and strong countenances.

Henderson shook hands with everybody including the Indians.

The Indians did not speak English and there was an interpreter. Dawson Nantuk started to break down.

Jim Nantuk said — "Tell my mother that her son Jim died bravely." He told his brother "There is no use crying. We have got to die and we might as well die bravely."

Hoods were put on them. Sheriff Harper's eyes were bent upon the watch he held and as its hands indicated eight o'clock he gave the hangman an almost imperceptible signal. Instantly the trap was open and the three veiled figures shot down a distance of six feet. There was a thud as the ropes felt the weight of the bodies and the structure shook with the strain. Not a word was spoken by anyone.

§

The report on the hanging stated that two died instantly, but there was a gruesome detailed description of Dawson Nantuk's death struggles. Finally, a black flag was hoisted to the flagpole to inform the crowd outside that the executions had taken place. The three were buried in graves inside the barrack grounds.

From Kittens to Mittens

As entrepreneurs hustled to make their money, it was possible to buy almost anything in Dawson, but some vendors had an unusually sharp eye for what would sell. Few would have thought that a litter of kittens would be much sought after, but one man thought otherwise. He brought the small pets to lonely people and the kittens also had the appealing advantage of being able to attack the ever-present rodent problems in Dawson.

The kitten story, an advertisement of a giant sale of clothing, the description of the largest nugget found in the Yukon and word of the first brick building to go up in Dawson were among the subjects dealt with by the *Nugget* as 1899 reached the shortened days of September.

THE KLONDIKE NUGGET   August, 1899

Pricey Kittens

All sorts of things have been brought to Dawson to tempt the unsophisticated miner to part with his hoard of gold, but it remained for a man named Bjerrenark, who returned from outside one day last week, to bring in a cargo of kittens. He showed a faithful knowledge of the Klondike market for the nice sleek striped kittens he brought in were worth exactly an ounce of dust.

§

THE KLONDIKE NUGGET   August, 1899

Advertisement
Mammoth 20th Century Enterprise
$65,000 in Stock for Sale on Front Street
Jack Kline Manager.
Prices 75% Less Than Ever Before in Yukon Territory
Hudson Bay blankets, 12 to 14 pounds - $10
All wool Fancy Tweed Suits, $15;
All Wool Shirts and Drawers, $3.50 a suit;
Fancy Percale Shirts, 75 cents; caps, 50 cents;
Black and Tan Dongola Shoes, $2.50 to $5;
All Moosehide Moccasins, $2.50

§

THE KLONDIKE NUGGET   September, 1899

Record Nugget

The largest nugget found in the Yukon up to date weighs 72 1/2 ounces and is worth $1,158. The existence of the nugget only became known Friday when Peter Jord brought it to town. The nugget is almost six inches long by nine inches and it is oblong in form. It is gold but the percentage of quartz — about six ounces — only makes it the handsomer specimen. It is indeed a beautiful object to look upon. It was at Claim No. 34 at Eldorado. Jord said he uncovered the piece in bedrock and struck it twice with his pick before he got it out. Big Alex McDonald was a part owner of the claim. Jord, a Dane, cached it away and sold it.

§

THE KLONDIKE NUGGET   September, 1899

First Brick Building

It makes Dawson decidedly metropolitan to see bricks piled up in front of a new arising edifice. Dawson's new brick building is going up on Third Street between Third and Fourth Avenue, near the Nugget office. It is destined undoubtedly to prove the progenitor of a long and illustrious line of brick buildings and as an ancestor of such premises merits public and respectful notice. In the future storage of perishable goods, it will go so far next winter towards making living endurable in Dawson.

§

STEELE OF THE NORTHWEST MOUNTED POLICE

If there was unanimity among the men and women who covered the events in Dawson, it concerned the men of the Northwest Mounted Police who merited respect, keeping law and order and Dawson under control.

One writer who was particularly impressed wrote of these men, making $1.25 a day in the midst of fortunes and free spending with $50 bottles of champagne and $10,000 bets on the turn of a card: "Their measured tramp shook the crowded sidewalks, their spurs jingled through the blare of dance halls, their shadows glided through lonely, dark and threatening lanes. Tact always used, violence only when they had to...."

These were the men who by their performance, dedication and gallantry laid the foundation of today's Royal Canadian Mounted Police, the scarlet-coated Mounties. One who achieved great fame across Canada was Sam Steele.

When a cross-section of the people in the rough-and-ready mining town turned out to praise the leading policeman and ask that he not be transferred out, it became obvious that he was quite a remarkable man. Samuel B. Steele was exactly that. A veteran Mountie, he had made his name on the prairies in his dealings with Indians and in his crackdown on the bootleggers and others who preyed on the tribes. He was tough, he was fair, he was incorruptible.

Some in Dawson chafed at his strict interpretation of the law, but they respected the man and obeyed his dictates with a minimum of rancour and trouble.

The government had decided to move Steele out because he had clearly established the rule of law in Dawson. It was not always applied as in other Canadian towns and cities, but it was what was best for the isolated, unique town of Dawson. Officialdom had other plans; Steele was chosen to raise a cavalry regiment — the Lord Strathcona Horse — for action in South Africa's Boer War. Several of the young Mounties went from the icy Yukon to the burning veldt to serve. Steele became a general in the First World War and was given a knighthood for his services. He died in 1919. This is what the businessmen, the miners, and the professional men of Dawson and the Yukon thought of him, as reported by the *Nugget*:

THE KLONDIKE NUGGET   August, 1899
Don't Go Steele

On last Saturday night at the Criterion Hall there was a public mass meeting of the residents of the district requesting Mr. Sifton, the Minister of the Interior, to revoke his order for removing Lieut. Col. Steele from his present position as commandant of the NWMP and member of the Yukon Council. The hall was crowded. When the meeting was called to order there was barely standing room. Most everyone of local prominence was there.

Though it was Saturday night the merchants gave their stores in charge of their clerks and turned out in force. The miners came in from the creeks, lawyers and doctors were present; in fact every occupation and profession was fully represented. If Mr. Sifton could have seen that business like body of men as they were assembled, if he could have heard the applause every word which was uttered in praise of Col. Steele received, if he could have seen and listened to the small groups of men which formed before and after the meeting and discussed most seriously the recall of the Colonel and the possibility of a favorable response to their petition, he would have realised he had made a grevious mistake in issuing his recent order.

Mr. Gibson was asked to voice the sentiments of citizens of the United States. "None can regret more sincerely the removal of Col. Steele than the Americans. We fully appreciate his eminent ability and impartial interpretation and administration of his duties."

§

THE FINAL DAYS OF '99

As the 19th century drew to a close, life in Dawson continued at its own pace, the important things always a little unusual, the people and events unique to this community.

THE KLONDIKE NUGGET   September, 1899

Costly Glass

One of the best illustrations I know of the conditions which prevail in Dawson is provided by a recent incident of Monte Carlo living. One of the recently arrived young women of the stage proclivities acquired a suite of rooms overhead, the former occupant being invited to move. When the new occupant moved in with an armful of personal belongings she was surprised to find the dispossessed girl engaged in removing the glass from the windows. Expostulation brought out the fact that the valuable glass was really the property of the departing girl as much as the tapestries of the room.

§

THE KLONDIKE NUGGET   October, 1899

River Closing

With the possible exception of a few of the small boats, all the steamboats navigating between Dawson and Whitehorse have started their last trips. Although the river is higher now than it was at this time last year still there is not sufficient water in which to turn the large boats. The Reindeer is still aground about 30 miles above Selkirk and the possibility of her arriving in Dawson this year is very remote. According to Mr. Campbell, Captain of the Ora, some 25 scows and barges, heavily loaded, are hung up on various bars between here and Whitehorse and 60 more are en route.

§

THE KLONDIKE NUGGET					October, 1899

Advertisement
Dr. Bourke's Hospital
Construction, equipment and staff equal to any
Scientifically heated to maintain equable temperatures
Trained nurses in attendance, inspection invited.
Terms from $10 a day including medical attendance.
Cow's milk and other delicacies requested by patients administered.

§

The events of November and December, 1899, gave little hint of the growing exodus from the community of Dawson.

THE KLONDIKE NUGGET					October, 1899

Advertisement
Now Open to the Public
Brand's New Club, Bath and Gymnasium
30 Finely Furnished Rooms
The Only Haven of Cleanliness this Side of Civilization
Department for Ladies
Open Night and Day
Third Avenue Between Third and Fourth Streets

§

THE KLONDIKE NUGGET					November, 1899

First Public School
The Catholic Church has the distinction of opening the first public school in the Yukon Territory. The building is a commodious one storey structure 30 feet by 40 and stands at the corner of First Avenue and Ninth Street. It is finished with desks, seats and blackboards and

could accommodate comfortably 40 pupils. The school was opened with 18 pupils in attendance with ages ranging from six to 14. There are 10 boys and 8 girls.

§

THE KLONDIKE NUGGET   November, 1899
Extra (front page headlines)
British Meet Defeat
Boers are Victorious in the Orange Free State
A British Attack Force Compelled to Withdraw
In the Hills They Are Surrounded and Mowed Down
The Boer Marksmanship is Producing High Casualties
Suffered by the British
Large Reinforcements Now En Route

§

THE KLONDIKE NUGGET   November, 1899
13 Scandinavians
The God of Fortune has dealt kindly with Scandinavians in the distribution of Cape Nome prizes. News comes from the new diggings that 13 of this sturdy nationality secured that number of successive claims on Onvail, perhaps the richest creek.

§

THE KLONDIKE NUGGET   December, 1899
Coldest Day
This very well was the coldest time of the present winter, mercury being reported from several places on the creeks and the Yukon River as having gone as low as 50 below zero. The result of the cold was much suffering on the part of teamsters who were freighting on the river with sleds.

§

CHRISTMAS BAZAAR

The ladies of the town organized the St. Mary's Bazaar at Christmastime in aid of hospital charity. The event was staged in the Grand Theatre which was "handsomely" decorated for the occasion. There was a fish pond and various stalls found at all such events, and the orchestra of the Yukon Field Force provided music for the ball.

It was a bright and glittering event that was very well attended and widely reported in the *Nugget*. It cleared about $14,000 for charity. This was the dinner menu on December 25, 1899 as reported by the *Nugget*. They went all out for this Christmas feast:

THE KLONDIKE NUGGET   December, 1899

Christmas Feast

Soup	-	Cream of Oyster
Fish	-	Grayling au gratin
Salad	-	Mayonnaise of Lobster
	-	Potato a L'Anglaise
Entrees	-	Boiled Leg of Mutton, caper sauce
	-	Braised Moose aux champignons
	-	Oyster Patties
	-	French Toast with Sauce
Roasts	-	Turkey with cranberries

	-	Leg of Pork with apple sauce
	-	Loin of Beef, pan gravy
Vegetables	-	Mashed Potato
	-	Sweet Corn
	-	Parsnips in Cream
	-	Sweet Potato
Dessert	-	Pumpkin and Mince Pie
	-	Plum Pudding
Cheese, Wafers		
Tea and Coffee		

§

There is one final note from the *Nugget* in December.

THE KLONDIKE NUGGET   December, 1899

Costly Heating

C. C. Kelly, one of the proprietors of the Monte Carlo saloon, club room and theatre, is authority for the statement that the bill for wood consumed as fuel at the place last week was $240, enough money to supply an eastern town of 2,000 population with fuel for the same length of time. But the Monte Carlo is in Dawson where wood is wood and where mercury has the playful habit of retreating to the cellar.

§

THE NUGGET EXPRESS

If *The Klondike Nugget* was a gold mine for Gene Allen, the Nugget Express unfortunately became a great, big, yawning hole into which he poured money. Allen, who had hardly put a foot wrong since landing in Dawson with only a pocketful of change, missed the signs that the boom days were gone and that Dawson was dying. Or, maybe he just didn't want to believe them.

In late '98, the winter-time transportation links into Dawson were poor. There were lots of freighters now in the business but service was spasmodic and inefficient. Allen had always been upset with mail delivery and so, letting go his tight hold on the paper, he started the Nugget Express delivery service. His dog teams carried small packages, mainly between business enterprises.

Soon the Express was a common sight in the mining community. With his usual enthusiasm, Allen poured his money into it. The Klondike had been good to him. Eighteen months or so after arriving, he had grossed more than a quarter-million dollars from his paper and express service, much more than most of those who had hoped to hack a fortune from the ground.

Allen was cocky and confident. His expansion plans were bold and expensive. He opened offices and hired a large staff in Dawson, Grand Forks which was on the main trail from Eldorado, Skagway, Seattle and several other places. No expense was too great.

In order to get the best dogs in the north for his teams, Allen paid as much as $200 for a dog, a huge price even in those free-wheeling days. He had dreams of a world-wide express service. In the fall of '99 he deeded the *Nugget* in its entirety to his brother, George, for a dollar.

Then his freight service began slipping. What really did him in was a more ambitious undertaking. A Seattle man had invented a wood-burning machine that produced steam to thaw the ground in the search for gold. Up to that time wood was burned directly on top of the frozen earth. When a few feet had been softened, the soil was dug out and as a shaft was developed the fire was relit in order to thaw a new section. The steam process was a revolutionary move in mining. Allen undertook to have 22 machines delivered to the Klondike before freeze-up. The heavy machines were moved out of Seattle to Skagway, but there was traffic congestion as suppliers rushed to beat winter. Allen hired scows to move them through the regular water route to Dawson and demand for the scows boosted the price from $400 to $1,200 each. Troubles piled up. Ice moved in. He hired crews of men at huge expense to help break the ice and move the scows through some frozen areas. Costs soared.

Allen was as good as his word and the machines were triumphantly delivered to the claims to which they were assigned. But at what cost?

Good old Gene had lived up to his word as the miners expected he would, but it cost him more than $40,000 to make good the contract and deliver the machines.

When Gene Allen started the Nugget Express, he paid top prices for his dogs to ensure fast delivery. (PHOTO BY E.A. HEBB, FROM THE KLONDIKE NUGGET, BY RUSSELL BANKSON.)

With the dawning of 1900, Allen knew that he was running out of money. Like so many entrepreneurs of more recent times, he was badly over-extended at the bank. He had spent money investing in a freight operation at a time when the bloom was fading and the Klondike was slowing down. He had also relinquished the reins of the *Nugget* and no longer had revenue from that source.

His career came crashing down in February, 1900, with the arrival of a telegram from Seattle. It stated simply: "Overdraft called. Credit stopped." That stopped the Express in its tracks. Allen was finished and on the last day of the month he sat in his room wondering what to do next.

In his biography, Allen tells a rather fanciful story of his last day in Dawson with a generous amount of self-pity. He still revelled in his standing with the miners, although it is doubtful he actually was "their champion or their idol," but there is no doubt he had championed their causes. It was ironic that Allen, who had tried to dissuade others from leaving Dawson and heading to Nome, thought that maybe, just maybe, he could repeat his success. He was the eternal optimist. He turned everything over to his lawyer, made an assignment of all he possessed and carefully listed every asset.

Then he told of a final visit to the Monte Carlo and a boisterous meeting with a group of friendly miners. He had laid out his last couple of dollars in a saloon when he first hit Dawson, and he put 50 cents from his dwindling resources on a card at the faro bank as he was about to leave. He also walked over to the Northern to mingle with friends for the last time, they being unsuspecting of what he was about to do. Allen then went looking for a young man named Bert Finney who had expressed a desire to join the Nome stampede but who didn't have the money for equipment. He gave Finney his gold pouch and told him to buy four good dogs and complete equipment for two for a 60-day winter run over the icy rivers to Nome: 1,500 very rugged miles in sub-zero temperatures. They set out just after midnight. Pulling out some of the prose with which he had delighted *Nugget* readers since the heady days of the trail of '98, Allen wrote in his diary that he stopped the team and looked back from the frozen Yukon River. "The moon was lighting the sky, glistening on the snow, throwing the ragged outlines of the city I had come to love up there in the shadow of the Arctic Circle into black silhouettes. I could see the thin columns of smoke rising straight and high above the buildings. I could almost hear the singing and the laughter and the talking of those thousands who believed in me, who trusted me, who were my friends. I'll make good! Nobody will lose an ounce because of me. When I get down to Nome I'll make a big cleanup. Then I'll bring it back here."

But it wasn't to be.

THE FINAL YEARS OF THE *NUGGET*

Gene was gone, but his brother George still owned *The Klondike Nugget* and it continued to publish. By the time 1902 rolled around, Dawson as a city and a community was much improved. There were more solid buildings; a city council provided local if controversial government; the telegraph line linked the Yukon with the outside and limited the feeling of isolation; social services including a well-run public school system were in operation; the White Pass and Yukon Railway between Skagway and Whitehorse, one of the world's great engineering feats, beat the passes and improved travel; and new laws had put a curb on gambling and some of the wilder excesses of Dawson life.

Nevertheless, there was the inescapable fact, for those who wanted to think about it, that Dawson was dying. The prospectors and miners were leaving as new strikes were reported. Some Klondike claims were considered worked out, although, many years later, the same claims were still producing gold that simpler, earlier methods couldn't recover. Gold production was declining every year and other business activity reflected it.

None of this was evident from reading the *Nugget* which still maintained that Dawson's future was unlimited. While it never indulged in figures, it is obvious that the paper's circulation was falling off as the population declined and advertising decreased. The *Nugget* now welcomed improvement in mail services and reported on doings in city council, Indian crafts, Dawson's generosity at benefit concerts, increasing mechanization in the mining industry, the coronation of a British king, and a little skulduggery.

In an inspired promotion, probably an attempt to attract new readers, the *Nugget* offered a $50 prize for the best song submitted in praise of the Yukon. It is debatable whether the song was as inspired as the promotion and it is doubtful that many sat around the campfires on the creeks singing "Yukona" which was the title of the prize-winning number. The paper printed both the music and the words. The $50 prize was split by Emogene Coleman, who had to take responsibility for the words, and Arthur Boyle to whom the music was attributed. The song was first heard at a choral concert at which Mr. Boyle was the choir director and Miss Coleman a chorister. The *Nugget* told its readers that Yukona "made a deep impression upon everyone who has heard it and is so thoroughly characteristic of this Yukon that it will undoubtedly live as long as the Yukon Territory is capable of maintaining a population." Unfortunately this wasn't the case.

Of course, it was the paper's $50, but to show its objectivity the *Nugget* quoted a story from the rival *Daily News* to gather fans for the song. The story stated: "A number in last night's program at the Choral concert requires and deserves special attention. It consisted of a song composed by one of the singers, a Miss Emogene Coleman, of a patriotic nature and set to music by Mr. Arthur Boyle, the director of the concert. Let it be known at once that the song and music are not to be criticized. It is doubtful if any one present was conscious of any feeling but one of sincere admiration, and the applause at the end of the five stanzas was as spontaneous and noisy as that heard at the political meetings in the same hall a few days ago."

The reporter went on to say that Emogene was very shy and hesitated to come forward until the applause reached a crescendo and Mr. Boyle took her hand and moved to centre stage. He referred to the words as "true poetry" and the music set to the poem by Mr. Boyle and sung by the full choir as "of a hymnal character, as it behooves a national or patriotic song to be. It moves with the majestic evenness of one of those hymns, which, like 'Nearer My God to Thee,' has taken possession of the worshippers of the world."

Miss Coleman and Mr. Boyle were praised for developing such a suitable song as appropriate to "the country beyond the border as it is for this Territory." This comment was probably made because Miss Coleman was an American.

It can be understood why the *Nugget* would print a story from a rival newspaper when the final paragraph of the item is taken into account.

The closing read: "Without doubt the song will soon be as familiar to the ear of the residents of the Yukon as are the strains of 'The Maple Leaf Forever.' Miss Coleman is to be complimented, as is Mr. Boyle, in having entered into the spirit of the poem in such an able manner."

Unfortunately, "Yukona" didn't top the hit parade in Dawson or anywhere else in 1902 and mercifully disappeared from sound. Without doubt, the words had something to do with it.

> All hail, all hail the Yukon
> Mighty, rich and glorious
> We seeking came,
> Content remain
> O'er fiercest gale victorious.
>
> {Chorus:
> Land of the Yukon;
> Hail, hail to thee,
> Land of the Yukon.
> Wide flows thy harmony.}
>
> Deep music of the ocean
> And harmony of hills
> United sing -
> The chorus ring -
> Till earth in gladdest answer thrills.
>
> {Chorus}
>
> So priceless are thy treasures
> Storehouses vast and deep
> Thy rocks bring forth
> Thy sands unfold
> God's sowing full and rich we reap.
>
> {Chorus}
>
> All forward as the Yukon
> Moves unto the sea
> Battling for right -
> For wisdom's light -
> Our blinded, fettered strength to free.
>
> {Chorus}
>
> O God here bless, our Yukon.
> Its stalwart sons command

> Thy wisdom, lend -
> In love to blend -
> Thy mighty country rich and grand.
>
> {Chorus}

The *Nugget* told its readers: "It is hoped that the song will be learned especially by the children. Copies will be sent to the Forks and other centres in the mining district and also to Forty Mile, to Whitehorse and other points along the river where any number of people reside. Yukona has been received with great favor by all who have heard it sung and is especially impressive when rendered by a large number of singers as was the case at the concert Friday night."

Despite the *Nugget*'s efforts, its $50 prize and the work of the team of Coleman and Boyle, "Yukona" was a gonna!

Gene Allen was no longer with the *Nugget*, but his fiery style could still be fanned into roaring flames as writers waxed indignant over some wrong as they saw it. No phrase was too damning and in their best blood-and-guts style, everything was black or white. The *Nugget* was at its best in a row over the upcoming civic elections. Where today would you read of the nefarious doings and the "merciless proclivities of a horde of office-seeking anthropophagi"? (A dictionary defines the word "anthropophagi" as man-eaters or cannibals.)

THE KLONDIKE NUGGET   January, 1902

> The Law Triumphs Over Corrupt Methods
> Justice Dugas Decides that Supplementary
> Voters' List is Illegal
> Kid Committee Receives a Body Blow from
> Which it Will Not Recover
> Attempts to Debauch the Voter Franchise Ends
> In Total Failure
> Taxpayers Seek the Protection of the Courts
> Against Bare Faced Efforts to Debauch
> The Voters' List

The ambitious Kid list had the coup de grace administered to them this morning in a way that warms the hearts of the solid citizens and taxpayers of this city whose interests have narrowly escaped the efforts of a gang of political shysters to feed and fatten the supplementary voters' list about which there has been so much contention. Their bid failed because it had not been prepared according to the provisions of the ordinance, because it was known to contain fictitious names and hundreds of others that had not the faintest shadow or title to right to exercise the franchise, and particularly because of the brand of the Kid committee which in itself was sufficient to condemn it. It has been knocked out, declared illegal, and will not constitute a part of the voters' list containing the names of those who will be entitled to vote in the election next Thursday. The preservation of the sacred right of the people to say who and by whom they will be governed, and not be turned over to the merciless proclivities of a horde of office-seeking anthropophagi is due to the fairness and wisdom of the Hon. Mr. Justice Dugas.

§

The reporter's salvo was bolstered by a blistering editorial in the best *Nugget* style. It stated:

THE KLONDIKE NUGGET   January, 1902
Editorial

The taxpayers and the voters of this town are confronted by a situation, the importance of which, some of them do not appear to appreciate. A fight is being made for the control of the voters' affairs by a gang of corruptionists who will stop at nothing to accomplish their nefarious purposes.

The ring leader of this gang has openly declared that he will ruin every man in Dawson who is the owner of property and that he will carry out his intention if the slightest opportunity of doing so is presented. Of this there can be no doubt.

It is the expressed purpose of the mob to secure possession of the tax levying power of the property holders who will be forced to pay the bills while favorites of the gang who have not a dollar of property at stake will be placed in positions of authority.

§

In another burst of outrage, the *Nugget* pointed out that of the 17 members of the Kid committee almost a third paid nothing in city taxes, while the others paid only $1,641.62. On the other hand, the 17 members of the Taxpayers Committee paid a total of $34,303, although it had to be noted that companies kicked in $12,000 of the amount. Despite the *Nugget*'s best efforts, the Kid committee prevailed, and after much political jockeying the *Nugget* finally approved the choice of mayor.

THE KLONDIKE NUGGET   January, 1902
           Amusement This Week
Auditorium Theatre: Tonight and continuous every night this week — "Arizona" — the great drama of western life.

Scotch Concert: On Wednesday night, proceeds will be given to the Presbyterian Church on Mission Street. Starting at 8 o'clock.

Juvenile Minstrels: On Wednesday night the Juvenile Minstrels will give a repetition of their former production at the New Savoy Theatre on First Avenue. Commencing at 8:30 p.m.

§

While delivery of the mail, other than during a postal strike, would not make news in today's world, the *Nugget* found a delivery of 500 pounds something to write about in the Dawson of 1902.

THE KLONDIKE NUGGET   January, 1902
           More Mail Coming
A consignment of 500 pounds of mail left Ogilvie this morning and should be in Dawson by the time this is seen by the Nugget readers as the trail is in fine condition and weather favorable to making good time. A large mail for the outside was despatched from the Post Office this morning and should reach Whitehorse in several days. The recent severe weather had done away with all the danger of weak ice and from now on there should be no excuse for from 10 to 15 days being consumed in transporting mail between the two terminals.

Two years ago when Tom Davies was looking after mail with such carriers as Louis Cardinal, Cook and other half-breed carriers, the distance from Dawson to Bennett was covered in four days and 17 hours, but then no freight was carried.

§

Dawson from the outset was a place of clubs, lodges, societies, associations and fraternal organizations covering a great many interests. For lonely people these groups provided a feeling of belonging and, of course, it was necessary to create one's own leisure-time activities other than joining in the action at the saloons, dance halls and theatres.

These groups got good coverage in the *Nugget* and eventually the paper came up with its own society columnist, a lady who for reasons of her own wrote under the name of Chappie. She seemed to be everywhere and no social event, no matter how small, was complete unless it got attention from her.

THE KLONDIKE NUGGET   February, 1902
Society News

The Bachelors' Dancing Club will entertain again Monday at the Pioneer Hall and this time will depart from the usual prosaic somewhat by giving a fancy dress ball. The costumes to be worn are being kept a secret, a great and tall secret, and not even the shrewdest diplomacy and persuasion being sufficient to induce the ladies to let known the costumes they will assume, and it is thought the affair will be one of the most enjoyable of the season. There will doubtless be Juliets, Violas, Queen Marys and what not, and only the presence of the gentlemen in costumes selected with equally good taste will be necessary to make the picture complete. The Club is considering the advisability of giving a cotillion before the beginning of the Lenten season.

Last evening John Heath gave a sleigh party in honor of his birthday. One of the stages of the Dawson Transfer and Storage was engaged and the party went to Bonanza where the temperature dropped as far as 41 Below where refreshments were enjoyed.

Mrs. Charles Malcolm is giving a ladies' euchre party this evening.

§

This also was Chappie:

THE KLONDIKE NUGGET   March, 1902
Society News

I dropped into the rink Monday evening and for a few moments was highly interested by the efforts of a young man endeavoring to waltz on skates. He looked very awkward and instead of taking one step for every beat of the music he only did so on every alternate bar. Then, too, he was unable to reverse which in a few moments made his fair partner so dizzy that she could hardly stand.

§

The *Nugget* gave its readers a good balance of local, national and international news. After the telegraph line was completed, outside news was current and not stale. The paper recognized the large number of Americans among its readers and presented a cross-section of what was happening in the lower 48. This was the stark story of another era in the South:

"Dear Little Nugget"

THE KLONDIKE NUGGET							February, 1902
Negroes in Trouble
Member of the Minstrel Company Got Gay
At Madrid, Miss., the Audience Raided
The Stage and Lynched Offender

During the performance last night of Richards and Pringle's Negro Minstrels, an altercation arose between members of the company and persons in the audience during which the stage was raided.

One of the minstrels used a revolver and several unimportant injuries were inflicted. It was subsequently learned that a negro named Louis Wright had done the shooting and he was arrested and taken to jail.

An hour later the jail was raided and Wright was taken out and lynched. The other members of the company were badly beaten and many got out of town.

§

In addition to serious affairs, the problems of day-to-day living in Dawson continued to warrant *Nugget* attention.

The purity of the drinking water was almost always on the minds of its citizens. One company capitalized on the concern in an advertisement which appeared in 1902:

THE KLONDIKE NUGGET							March, 1902
Advertisement
When the Thaw Commences

Do not jeopardize your good health by taking into your system germs and disease. We have placed the price of our mineral waters at such a figure that they are not a luxury but a necessity. Shasta Water, 50 qts case, $20; Apollinaris Water, 100 pts. case, $30; genuine imported Belfast Gingerale, 10 doz. pts. $20.

Northern Commercial Company

§

THE KLONDIKE NUGGET							March, 1902
Cream is Monarch — Over all it Surveys in Dawson
Price May Advance as High as $20 per Case

Cream, cream, cream is king in Dawson today and before the opening of navigation bids fair to become an absolute monarch. Cream has been on the rise for the past two months and now is hard to find at $15 per case. To the purchaser at retail prices, three cans are now given for $1 where earlier in the season the same dollar would have purchased five cans.

Various reasons are given for the jump in prices among which may be the fact that the demand has been growing this winter more than ever before. In the early fall cream was best and everybody used it. Palates which previously had been content to put up with common, ordinary condensed milk acquired an appetite for cream and that appetite must be satisfied.

Cream. How long before the arrival of the first boat?

§

A major headline in 1902 heralded the end of the Boer War in South Africa. The war had created divisions in Dawson — most Canadians of British origin backed the army of the monarchy against the settlers of Dutch ancestry; most Americans backed those whom they felt were the victims of colonization. Among those who served on the British side, and some of those who fell, were young members of the Northwest Mounted Police who had eagerly volunteered for the excitement of the war in the veldt.

However, much of the news centred on local issues which had not changed much since the *Nugget* began publishing.

THE KLONDIKE NUGGET   March, 1902

Scarlet Women are Scattered Around Town
Most of Them are Running Cigar Stores
Many Complaints Made

A complaint has been made of the fact that scarlet women of the town are scattered around the residential district and are not confined to any particular locality.

They have been returning to the city now and may be found in a number of localities where they invariably represent themselves as running cigar stores or confectionery stores.

It is generally recognized that a drastic ordinance forbidding their presence in the city would accomplish nothing as they would find some means of evading the law.

Although it may be impossible to abolish the evil, said the businessman, it might be controlled and kept from flaunting itself before the public eye.

§

The arrival of spring and the breakup of ice on the rivers was always the most anticipated annual event in Dawson. Even though news now reached the community rapidly from all over the world, travel in and out remained difficult and spring breakup brought with it anticipation and excitement.

THE KLONDIKE NUGGET　　　　　　　　　　　　　　　May, 1902

The First Steamer Arrives
After Seven Months of Desolation and Quietude
The Waterfront again Becomes a Scene of Activity
Heavy Mail Received
How Ice Jams Were Avoided
Few Passengers — Perishable Freight and Livestock

It was nearly five when several who were on the lookout for the first sight of steamboats saw a puff of smoke arising far up the bend beyond Klondike City. The cry of "Steamboat" was raised and the ubiquitous street gamins took it up and half the houses of the city emptied themselves, everyone rushing down to the waterfront to greet the craft so welcome. Seemingly within five minutes every dock was black with people and as the first boat appeared and tooted a merry good evening there was a yelling and cheering loud enough to awaken the dead.

§

The first football game of 1902 was a spectacle observed by only a few residents of Dawson. The reasons for the small attendance are aptly described in the *Nugget*.

THE KLONDIKE NUGGET　　　　　　　　　　　　　　　June, 1902

Football Pleasure
First Game of the Season Last Night
Canadians Wallop English
By a score of 32 - 1
Slow Game

The Canadian giants literally wiped up the earth with the Sons of Old England on the football gridiron last night, the score at the conclusion of the game standing at 32 - 1 in favor of the former. It was the first game of the season and on account of the rain the attendance was small but those who were there enjoyed the rare spectacle of seeing 30 men wallow about in mud for an hour.

The ground was too soft and slippery for fast play and there was little attempt at team work, no practice having been indulged in before the game.

To those accustomed to the collegiate game such as is played in the States, the rugby game seems tame in the extreme by comparison. There are no mass plays, no line bucking, no holes made for the quarter to crawl through, no interference, no signals by which the team that has the ball knows the play that is to be attempted and no one knows what is to come next until some player grabs the ball and starts to sprint. Then too, rugby lacks the ginger of the collegiate game. It isn't as fast and the ball too often is not in play.

§

This was not an era without feeling or compassion, but it was a time when a paper could report that people with mental illness had "wheels in their heads." This story in the spring of 1902 didn't hesitate to list the names of seven people who were being taken to a medical centre in New Westminster, B.C. Breakdowns were not uncommon as some gave in to loneliness, feelings of inadequacy, deprivation, physical illness, an inability to handle the swirl of life that was Dawson or maybe a combination of them all.

THE KLONDIKE NUGGET   June, 1902
Insanity Patients Will be Sent to New Westminster
Peculiar Hallucinations by One Imagining
Himself a Pugilist

One of the boats leaving for Whitehorse next week will bear as part of its cargo an interesting section of humanity. They are at present confined in the insane ward of the barracks, a number of people who are afflicted with wheels in their heads.

None are violent with the exception of Robert Sinclair and he can be easily handled by appealing to his peculiar dementia. He imagines himself a pugilist and as he has tremendous strength, he has made things interesting for his guards. His problem became effective last winter while at work on lower Dominion Creek. One of his ambitions is to have a go with Frank Slavin whom he promises to pulverize. When it was decided to bring him into town he was told a go had been arranged with Slavin and he would have to go into training. That satisfied him and he got onto the sled and caused no trouble except for his incessant chatter about uppercuts, left swings and right-hand hooks.

§

Frank Slavin was an Australian-born heavyweight boxer who took on all comers in Dawson rings and also dabbled in mining ventures.

"Dear Little Nugget"

The *Nugget* continued to be in the forefront of helping Dawson look after its own in times of need. It ran, probably free of charge, an announcement advertising a benefit in aid of a boy badly hurt. Local entertainers always were quick to donate their talents to worthy causes. Capital cities such as Ottawa are, in today's world, generally unloved by much of the surrounding country, but Dawson in 1902 even held a benefit for the far-away seat of federal government when fire razed a large part of that community.

THE KLONDIKE NUGGET   July, 1902
Tonight Tonight
Grand Benefit Tendered to Master Richfield Cameron
The Unfortunate Boy Who was Recently Crippled for Life
Kathleen Mavourneen Will be Presented
And a Large List of Specialty Acts.

The Auditorium stock company, the musicians of the city and all the leading vocalists and specialists have volunteered their services. Every dollar made goes to the boy. Come and see the best show ever given in Dawson and help a worthy cause. If you can't come, buy a ticket and send a friend. Tickets on sale at Rudy's drug store, Reid and Company and at the AB Hall box office.

§

There still were more Americans than Canadians or Britons in Dawson when the coronation of King Edward VII took place in distant London. Dawson was a bastion of the Empire, nonetheless, and it celebrated the event in grand style with a 21-gun salute and a Venetian fete along the waterfront. It seemed that everyone joined in, Uncle Sam's sons and daughters wishing all the best to the late Queen Victoria's son. His crowning had been delayed because of an operation for appendicitis.

THE KLONDIKE NUGGET   August, 1902
Observed in Dawson
Coronation Service and Sports
The City Generally is Dressed in Holiday Attire
Many People are Out

In honor of the coronation of Kind Edward VII, Dawson is today in holiday attire. Beautiful decorations are seen on every hand. Business of all kinds is suspended and on every face regardless of nationality is a look that betokens sanction to the phrase "God Save the King."

At 8:30 this morning there was a grand military parade of the North West Mounted Police and the Dawson Rifles to the Church of England where in the new building, which was crowded to capacity, the specially prescribed coronation services were conducted.

At 11 a.m. a game of baseball between two local teams.

Twelve o'clock, the Royal Salute, 21 guns were fired.

By 1:30 this afternoon, men, women and children from all parts of the city were wending their way to the barracks athletic grounds where at 2 p.m. began a carnival of sports in which both children and adults are participating.

At 8:30 this evening will occur a spirited lacrosse game between the "City" and the "Hardwares".

At 7:30 a half-mile handicap horse race will be run on First Avenue for a handsome silver cup valued at $150 and generously donated by jeweler J. L. Sile.

At 8 o'clock tonight will take place on the river front in front of the Fairview, a Venetian Fete and other aquatic sports and at 10:30 the day's celebrations close with a good display of fireworks.

In no place in King Edward's vast domain can a more perfect day be had for the coronation celebrations and festivities than is being accorded his subjects and their cousins in Dawson.

If no unexpected circumstances have arisen, King Edward VII has been crowned King of Great Britain and ruler of the mighty British Dominion beyond the seas. The event, though doubtless devoid of much of the pomp and pageantry that otherwise would have occurred, has acquired a universal interest by reason of the brave struggle that the King has waged against the grave illness by which he was so recently stricken.

The whole world has watched the progress of the King's illness and the news of his continuing improvement has been received with profound satisfaction wherever civilized man dwells.

In our small but entirely cosmopolitan community there are none who will not heartily and sincerely join with British subjects the world over in expressing a devout wish for long life to Britain's king.

§

The *Nugget* did not report a great deal on the local Indian population, but the native people did occasionally rate coverage. The entrepreneurship and craftsmanship of the Moosehead Indians was admired, although race relations again got short shrift when one writer assured his readers that no traits "of the Jew" showed in the Indians when it came to bargaining.

THE KLONDIKE NUGGET　　　　　　　　　　September, 1902
Indians Have a Thriving Basket Business
Fix Price and Stay With It

The Moosehead Indians are now reaping a small harvest from the sale of birchbark baskets. They are very adept in the manufacture of these baskets which they make in all sizes with capacity all the way from a quart to five gallons and these they sell at prices ranging from 50 cents to $3.

The Indian women are close bargainers and as old clothes constitute the chief article for which they exchange baskets in the way of barter, they are very close examiners of what they take in exchange. There are no traits of the Jew in Indians as when they state a price they stick to it.

§

Dawson and its citizens, as has been noted, were in the main quite generous in looking after those who had fallen on hard times largely through no fault of their own. However, as reflected by the *Nugget*, this was not the case for those who didn't want to work but preferred living on what they could steal or beg. When it was decided to take a hard line on vagrants, the "Big Royal Saws" referred to were those at the woodpile in the police barracks where prisoners often found themselves adding to the city's fuel supplies.

THE KLONDIKE NUGGET　　　　　　　　　　September, 1902
Many are Getting Out
Dawson No Longer Vagrants' Haven of Rest
Visible Means of Support Necessary
Or Big Royal Saws will be Provided

Within the past week a large number of men belonging to the undesirable class of "tell nots" that have infested Dawson ever since the fall of '97, departed Dawson for the outside.

When the steamers Tyrell and Columbia recently sailed on their special low-rate trips the police saw a number on board they could scarcely believe were leaving the country. But when they were asked to show their tickets they all read "Dawson to Whitehorse".

A few, however, have essayed to work a bluff by putting on overalls and going to the creeks in the guise of working men. This bluff has worked in the past with the result that it will not work again. The creek police have been notified to drive the vagrants from the creeks back to Dawson where they can be cared for in a way that will at least ensure them earning what they eat.

With the carrying out of the plans being mapped out, Dawson will be anything but a haven of rest this coming winter for people without visible means of support. "Visible means" in the shape of big, long, royal saws will be provided by the police.

§

Mechanization already had made itself felt in the creeks of the Klondike and it was clear that the miner with his pan, pick and shovel was giving way to giant machines that could scoop up great amounts of gravel and recover gold by new and vastly improved methods.

There were arguments, differing opinions and some uproar from the various interests, but headlines on a long article giving details of the mechanics and performance of various types of dredges and diggers told the story.

THE KLONDIKE NUGGET   September, 1902
Future Mining Operations to be Conducted
Upon a Gigantic Scale
New Methods of Handling Immense
Quantities of Gravel at Small Costs to be Introduced
Gold Output Will be Greatly Increased

§

In his report for the 1902 school year, Superintendent Ross described an improved system catering to close to 500 children at several schools, including even a high school division for Dawson's five oldest students.

It was unfortunate that after all the work that had gone into providing a sound operation for the young, it would be implemented for such a short time as the population declined and children and their parents moved out of Dawson. The system recognized its responsibilities. There are few parents in Canada today, if any, who get a monthly school report on their children, particularly covering such areas as "studies, punctuality, deportment and progress."

THE KLONDIKE NUGGET   February, 1903
Attendance at School
Parents to Have Monthly Report in Future
School Now Divided Into 5 Grades
With a High School Department
Superintendent of Schools, Ross, has just completed his report of the attendance at the public schools for the year. This shows that in all

schools the average attendance was 466 of which five are in the high school department.

The sexes are relatively evenly divided with 235 boys and 231 girls. The public schools are now divided into several grades and the average attendance of these grades is:

kindergarten — 89
1 — 152
2 — 78
3 — 105
4 — 80
5 — 9
high school — 5

Superintendent Ross will start on the first of each month to report to parents of the standing of their children. All children will receive a percentage for studies, punctuality, deportment and progress.

§

BOOM TO BUST

Dawson was a classic example of boom to bust. From a bustling, upstart town of about 30,000 in 1898 — the biggest community in Canada west of Winnipeg — it fell away and estimates put it at 7,000 in 1901, about 1,000 in 1921, and a near ghost town in following years. Old, deserted buildings collapsed, and streets that once were packed with men and women in pursuit of their hopes and dreams were taken back by the bush. It was simply because the easy-to-mine gold had been quickly scooped up: Eldorado, Bonanza, Hunker and the other creeks had been worked over by the first men on the spot.

It is not certain how much gold was taken from the Klondike, considerable quantities being quietly spirited away to avoid the much detested taxes. About $100,000 worth was mined near the Stewart River when the first men into the area started working the creeks in '85. There was the expansion following Carmack's strike in '96 and in '98 it is believed about ten million dollars were extracted. The peak year was 1900 when $24,000,000 in gold was shipped out — a massive sum in its time considering that the federal government budget for all of Canada in the same year was about $60,000,000. After that, the amounts nosedived sharply as claims were abandoned: considered worked out by the methods of the "gumboot" miners.

Gold mining was far from finished, but despite the introduction of mechanization and much improved methods, it never again came close to creating the fortunes that were made during the Klondike rush. In this new era emerged one of the most unlikely individuals to set foot in the Klondike, Arthur Newton Christian Treadgold, Oxford graduate, teacher, engineer, promoter and a direct descendant of Sir Isaac Newton. A tiny man who always favoured big bowler hats, he planned well and saw great possibilities for making fortunes.

He first came to Dawson in '98 in the guise of a journalist and sent eloquent descriptions of the flamboyant community to *The Manchester Guardian*. Because of his education and training as an engineer, he knew that in the low-rolling-hills separating the creeks there were massive quantities of "White Channel Gravels" that had been there for thousands of years and contained gold. Mechanized methods would be required, however, if the gold was to be recovered.

Hydraulic mining on a large scale would depend on a sure source of water and Treadgold moved to obtain control of much of the Klondike River. There were highly complex dealings involving mining laws, leases, claims, water rights, financing and much more. The scheming and the wheeling and dealing covered a range of interests and people from English financiers to the boxer, Frank Slavin.

Government lobbying also paid off and with the authority of the federal interior minister, Clifford Sifton, Treadgold was granted what became known as the Treadgold Concession. When word was posted in Dawson in early 1902 that the concession had finally been approved, the *Nugget* fumed: "What is known as the Treadgold Concession; the most colossal octopus that ever fastened its tentacles on the gold gravels of the Yukon Territory, again makes its presence felt."

And in an editorial in its best thundering style, the *Nugget* maintained: "Never before in the history of the Klondike and Yukon Territory has such a wave of righteous indignation swept over the country as that which is now stirring in the souls of every man and woman about the infamous order-in-council which gives to Treadgold and his fellows the right to all the vacant and unoccupied land on the largest creeks in this the richest spot on earth."

In response to charges of payoffs and corruption, Sifton maintained correctly that to keep Dawson and the Klondike thriving there had to be mining on a massive scale.

It was the lawyers who made the money as protest piled on protest. The federal government took a full blast; there was an enquiry and finally in 1904 the order was rescinded. Undaunted, Treadgold battled on in a series of complex manoeuvres, plots, alliances and partnerships involving financing from England and the United States, fighting and losing assorted battles and taking his interests to Canadian and British courts.

Mechanization did come to the Klondike; massive dredge shovels tore at the gravel and made money right up until it finally became unprofitable in 1966. Treadgold was in and out of the operations for years. Unbelievably, the mighty mite, the battling Treadgold — who had gold in his name and in his soul — didn't give up his many suits and actions until March 23, 1951, more than half a century after he first came to Dawson. He was contemplating raising more money to make an appeal to the House of Lords over some of his interests when he fell off a London bus and died shortly after in St. Bartholomew's Hospital. He was 87. Oxford graduate turned sourdough, Treadgold, like so many others who trekked to the Klondike, made his money, and lost it.

THE *NUGGET* CASHES IN

If the *Nugget* came in with a bang under the ebullient Gene Allen, it went out with a whimper. There was nothing in its pages to suggest that its demise was likely although those in Dawson possibly were aware of problems with a falling population, shrinking business activity and a drop in advertising revenue and readership.

While there was no such thing as a circulation audit then, the *Nugget* probably topped at about 2,000 copies daily. This was fairly respectable under the circumstances, given the population and the competition at one time from two other dailies. *The Yukon Midnight Sun*, the paper that Allen raced on the trails which later became simply *The Yukon Sun*, and the late-arriving *Dawson News* which didn't get into business until a year after its competitors, 1899, were the two other main papers to serve Dawson in these early years. The *News* outlasted both the others.

The *Nugget* was still 25 cents a copy (three dollars a month delivered anywhere along the creeks and in town) when a simple notice appeared on July 11, 1903, under the heading "Change of Ownership." It stated: "This will serve to inform the public that the Daily Klondike Nugget and Semi-Weekly Nugget, together with the plant, stock, fixtures, etc., of the two businesses have been sold to the Record Publishing Company."

The notice was over the name of George M. Allen, Gene's brother, the man who had accompanied Hickman and the dogs on the boat from Seattle five years before and who had helped manhandle the press and the other equipment over the White Pass, against the winter blizzards and along the lakes and down the rivers to Dawson.

When newspapers have folded in recent years — unfortunately too often in Canada and the United States — there has been much emoting, farewells from every section and sometimes some overly sentimental gushing from columnists. This could have been expected from the *Nugget* but it didn't happen.

Much of the sentiment expressed at the death of a newspaper is honest because to those who have worked on them, papers have been living things. There has been in great measure a loyalty and a desire to scoop the opposition that goes beyond the preservation of a pay cheque. Yet there was nothing in the *Nugget*'s final edition. Stroller White's column dealt with the joys of picnicking and one of the major stories covered a talk by visiting Commissioner Evangeline Booth, of Salvation Army fame, delivered in St. Andrew's Presbyterian Church. Another headline said the end approached for the pope who had lapsed into delirium after a bad night. There were no stories about this being the final edition of the *Nugget*.

In its short life, Dawson had seen a lot of papers come and go, most of them shortlived. Without doubt the most dashing was *The Dawson Daily Dagger and Theatrical Advertiser* which had a very short run in 1898.

Front Street, Dawson City, summer of 1903, when the Nugget *ceased publication.*
(COURTESY VANCOUVER PUBLIC LIBRARY, PHOTO 8262.)

Records are vague, but it seems that it only lasted a few editions. The same was the fate of some of the other publications that sprang up in Dawson at its peak, including: *The Dawson City Ranger, The Klondike Morning Times, The Klondike Miner and Yukon Advertiser, The Sunday Gleaner* and *The Klondike Miner*.

After absorbing the *Nugget*, the *Record* didn't last too long in a collapsing economy. It was taken over by *The Yukon Sun* in November of 1903, and shortly after that the *Sun* also set.

This left *The Dawson News* as the sole survivor of the papers that had informed, entertained, shocked, infuriated and delighted the people of Dawson and the creeks in those lonely, isolated days when there was no radio, no television and print reigned supreme.

For a long-time newspaperman it was somehow appropriate that death came to Gene Allen while he was helping organize the new Washington State Press Club. An obituary in *The Seattle Times* said a heart attack, suffered on the club premises, possibly resulted from over work in preparing for a visit to the Pacific Northwest that December of 1935 by a congressional party which included American Vice-President John Nance Garner.

The obituary stated that 67-year-old Allen was born in Oak Park, Illinois and was a graduate of the University of Kansas. He learned the printing trade in the Midwest and came to Seattle where he worked as a compositor. Then came 1897 and the great adventure of his life. After his northern experiences he went to Idaho where he was involved in the mining business and worked for *The Wallace Press Times*. He retired in 1926 and returned to the Seattle area where he was named to reorganize the old Seattle Press Club into a state-wide organization.

Allen's northern exploits lived with him for the rest of his life. He was an active member of sourdough organizations and pulled other old pioneers together when he set up the Tacoma Sourdough Club. He was survived by his widow, two sons and two daughters.

Three months earlier, in September, 1935, a heart attack also claimed the life of George Allen who was still in the newspaper business in Washington State. George, who had run the *Nugget* until its demise, was publisher of *The Toppenish Review* when he died at the age of 57. Raised in Seattle and ten years younger than his older brother, George was a graduate of the University of Washington. He also was survived by a widow and four children.

Both men were survivors of the trail of '98 and had tasted the heady wine in Dawson when it seemed all things were possible for all men. They were part of a bygone era that was never to be repeated.

In the mid-1990s the Yukon's population is about what Dawson's was at its peak in 1898, around 30,000. Dawson has rebounded from the worst of its decline and has climbed to about 2,000 people, including some of the approximately 1,000 men and women who still explore and mine gold and other minerals in the Yukon. Total mineral production in 1992 was close to a half-billion dollars but gold accounted for only about ten percent of the total.

Dawson and the Yukon today pin a lot of hope on the future of tourism in their vast and largely untamed land. There is air service, and the drive from Dawson to Whitehorse on an all-weather highway takes about six hours. The cabin where Robert Service, the bard of the Yukon, lived in Dawson can still be found.

The old Palace Grand Theatre, has been restored by the government and if you listen carefully you can hear the laughter of the ghosts, the squeals of the can-can dancers and the tinkle of gold on the barman's scale. You will not find any trace of the *Nugget*, although among the ghosts you may be able to identify Uncle Andy Young shouting, "The *Nugget*, the *Nugget*, the Dear little *Nugget*."

ENDNOTES

1. ALLEN'S NUGGET. Quotations are from *The Klondike Nugget* by Russell Bankson published in 1935 by Caxton Printers Ltd. of Caldwell, Idaho. Copies may be viewed in the condensed shelving section of the Vancouver Public Library, or the Special Collections Division, Allen Library, at the University of Washington in Seattle.
2. THE EARLY EDITIONS. This description of Bill Gates' arrival in Dawson is from *The Klondike Nugget* by Russell Bankson.
3. HOW THE WORLD SAW IT. Quotations are from an article in the periodical *National Historic Parks* by Hal Guest, published in 1978.
4. SALOONS. This description is from *The Klondike Nugget* by Russell Bankson.